Kaleidoscope

Kaleidoscope

You Already Are All You Need To Be,
Right Where You Are!

www.Kaleidoscopethebook.com

Kaleidoscope

Another Book by ShannonRae

Your Center, Your Power
Where You Connect to Peace, Power and Passion!

www.YourCenterYourPower.com

Kaleidoscope

Kaleidoscope

You Already Are All You Need To Be,
Right Where You Are!

www.Kaleidoscopethebook.com
ShannonRae

**The Power Integration Center
Las Vegas, NV**

Publication

The Power Integration Center
7380 S Eastern Ave #124-213
Las Vegas, NV 89123

Copyright 2004 – 2007
by The Power Integration Center

by ShannonRae
Manufactured in the United Sates of America

For information on bulk rates and purchasing
please contact
The Power Integration Center Directly at
www.powerintegrationcenter.com
760-455-2253
or sales@powerintegrationcenter.com

ISBN 978-0-6151-4404-7

Kaleidoscope

Acknowledgments

This book is dedicated to the spirit that lives inside of me. The force that guides me. The voice I have found by connecting to it. It is dedicated to the fire that keeps on burning in the face of trial and triumph. The fire that has burnt down houses so homes could be built.

This work is dedicated to all the people, especially women, in the world who choose to find and live the power they already have inside of themselves. May you all find and live your essence, connecting to the power burning in the center of yourself. May the power that exists in you right now create peace, power and passion in your life! May it be done on your terms.

This book is dedicated to the children, friends, family and community that have lived through my moments of power and my moments of subjection. It's dedicated to all those who have joined me on this grand journey of power. Just as we teach, it does take a village to grow. It took a village, a community of faithful souls, inspired by the mission of planetary peace, one individual at a time, to bring this work to fruition! May you all be as blessed as I have been along the way. May you all reap the seeds you've sown. May the world reap the gifts you have shared!

A special thank you to my sons Devin and Tyler, and my soul sisters Uzuri and Shannon, for all the support and sacrifices you made along the way and the faith you had when I couldn't find it myself.

Kaleidoscope

Considerations

A few things to keep in mind as you read this book, considerations if you will.

1. This is a non-spacial, shifty journey that's irreverent of "time". Get ready for an *Alice in Wonderland* expedition. That includes grammar that may, or may not, be typical or "proper". Remember in a time and space, where technically there is none, I ask you to release your limitations and allow yourself to simply flow moment to moment. Which may at times transition in ways that may not seem proper, typical or linear. Let it be what it is so it can take you where it needs to.

2. This story is not written in any chronological order. You will find yourself shifting from one point in life to another within in the story, which is kind of how our memories work when we get to the core. This story is organized in a flow of the message and encompassed in and around the feelings, which lead to the lessons and purpose of the experiences. This is ultimately the purpose of this book; to begin paying attention to the purpose, flowing with the process and pull back from the individual points in life to appreciate the individual moments more. Whenever you see a - shift. . .shift . . . - you can certainly be guaranteed you are shifting. Most frequently that also means within the story and the timeline. It may be forward, it may be backward, it may be neither, but it's always a shift.

3. There are rabbit holes within rabbit holes. Understand this is not a one time catch all read. It's a bit like a Bloomin' Onion. The layers will keep on

peeling, and peeling. Each time you read it, a new perspective will be present. With each new perspective another layer of wisdom will be revealed. Pick it up over and over again. Share it time and again. The wisdom it provides will cycle as you do. Keep on churnin'. . .

4. Triggers are buried within the pages, inside the stories, throughout the words and certainly contained in the truth. They were not necessarily intentional, but were certainly guided there. Those triggers will release a memory deep within you of a truth you've always known. Be aware of them. . . Some of them will trigger through love, others may trigger through fear. The feelings they evoke will be as vast and varied as the souls and personalities reading this book. Trust that the triggers, none-the-less, will bring you to a space of love and acceptance. They will bring you to the place of home.

5. You will notice several words with italics around them like – 'time'. Whenever you see a word like this it's an indicator that the word has several interpretations and I may not be speaking of it in a manner in which you commonly understand it. It may also indicate that there really is no word that will sufficiently describe that which I am speaking. It may, however, be the most commonly understood word and best word to use in order to keep the focus of this book and its readers. Either way let them be an awakening, a calling, to that which I speak.

6. Finally, honor yourself, as well as those around you as you cycle, and shift. Most of all, celebrate as you come on home.

Kaleidoscope

Chapters

This book isn't really written in chapters although there are clear and intentional transitions within 5 sections.

"Sections"

The Entry Way: What just might be a "beginning" of a cycle that technically has none.

The Scope of My Lens: Just what it says, the way I see and or saw it considering there is no "time".

The Point of Power: A bit of an exploratory on the point of power, it's cycle and it's process.

In Closing: My attempt at wrapping it up, and wrapping it around.

The Campaign 4 Truth: An experiment in perpetuation; intentionally creating an infectious virus of epidemic proportions.

Kaleidoscope

Kaleidoscope

Entry Way

Kaleidoscope

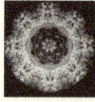

I was standing on the concrete balcony at the base of the tree house surrounded by some of the most loving and soulful friends I have ever had. The open, artistic flair, with which they embraced each other, and life, were awe inspiring. Not only in their vast and varied works of art, but also in their intimate touch of friendship. This was the treasure we were all celebrating together in a gathering that was all too common place; in the space we called the *Tree House*.

The drums were beating, the piano was humming and Shonda was singing. We were all dancing, moreover we were flowing. Flying high on the vibration of the spirit we were feeling. It's moments like this that are written about in books, watched on large screens and envisioned in meditations. That night the truth of the spirit seeped through the webs of our connection, taking us to our own rumination.

All of a sudden the chanting became howling from a place within me I had no idea subsisted. A sound so home it had come from centuries of moans. A bass that rose from the roots I had grown from. A reverberation that vibrated to the trees surrounding us and inspired the sounds of those around me to chant in unison, as our bodies moved to the spirit rising within us.

My body was loose. Every muscle flowed with a space throughout them, allowing a movement, like natures own howling wind, whipping through the trees of that very house. To imagine the flight of the birds high above in a sky so open with space is one thing. To feel the lift of the wind beneath your wings, rising from Mother Earth below, fully integrated with the forces of power, fluid in a wide open space that's utterly infinite; only the feeling gives witness to. The feeling, only an experience gives measure to.

My body, the mother of my own nature, opened up, revealing to me in that very moment, the feeling of my own expression of the power that is the life of us all.

We all have moments like this. Ones that open up a portal in our bodies giving way to the experience of spirit in unity with the place we are in, taking us to a space that is infinite. The kind that places us in a passionate power invoking a wholeness we can't always seem to hold around us, in the daily routine that seems to drown us. Moment to moment we might recite a Maya verse or connect to a Patti vibration of soulful song, few of us let those moments engulf our being consistently.

We may not always grab hold or dive straight into the axis. However, power, the kind found only in truth, will continually seduce us with her passionate flame, moment to moment, asking us to ignite the fire of power, of spirit, within us. Incite the life that is us, sharing that light with others, until the merging of it in me and you, and the ones to either side of us and those on the other side of them becomes all the experience there is.

Finding the voice that is our own, the chanting that vibrates the bones of our bodies, to a place of a home way deep down where our own roots began, brings the freedom of those moments to our daily lives; it brings the dance we so often find only in the solitude of our shower songs, to the daily vibration that we can carry amongst our steps.

Moments like those can be the very experience of our entirety, rather than sole moments of flames that blow in and out of the wind that sways us. Distant memories of an experience once had can become a life you lead when you open up to the truth of it and claim your space with it. The wind that sways you now can lift you to flight, moment to moment. The light that blinds you, can also guide you. It's the breathe you take, moment to moment, where you begin to know, own, live and share the power that you already are.

Why did it take getting lost in the spirit of that moment to chant the depth of my soul? To share the roots of my home in a baritone bass that even I had yet to experience? I found in that moment, the truth that every moment has the opportunity to share with me the power of the spirit within me. That every time I think I know it, as I connect to it, it has more life to share with me. And in that sharing it seethes through the essence of me onto the life that is me and into those around me. Until it all just merges into the love I am today.

> **Truth**
> Truth is only experienced. It's only communicated through the experience of sharing. My only intention is that the experience of my sharing in this book, the sharing of my perspective, of my moments through my scope, inspires you to be present to your own. That it inspires you to shed all that covers your power so you may share it passionately with others. And in that, continue to experience, and be witness, to the depth of life, its cycle of creation and all the glory "it", "we" are.

Standing there, tears streaming down my face, melting deeper into the carpet below me, praying to lose enough of me that I'd just blend into the surroundings beneath me . . .

"Daddy look at the new dress I got!" showing my prize new possession to the one who'd made me princess. Not a motion evoked, as he sat there reading the newspaper, while simultaneously watching the news.

Without missing a beat, or raising his head, he said, "Beautiful!" As if I was ignorant enough to miss he hadn't seen a thing, nor had his attention turned at all.

Standing there for enough minutes to think the surroundings just might swallow me whole, but not enough for him to turn his attention I swung for the closest door and the haul up stairs.

Tears still streaming, head hung and the dress now flung on the floor in the corner of the room while I ran to the corner of the closet just behind the dresser. The one place where I knew not a prayer was needed for the place to swallow me whole and lose me for at least a moment.

Moments are all we need. All we need to forget or remember our sense of power, our sense of self and the spirit that feeds it all. We go through millions of them in our lives. Millions like this one influenced by the surroundings we are immersed in.

Our power is always available to us, it is us. Moments like this give us the illusion that we have lost our power. That someone else may have taken it from us. As if it's something we lose or gain, something that is separate from us to begin with. Our perspective of this situation, and the

million other moments like it, will determine whether or not
we choose to embrace our power, or live the illusion that
we've handed it over to another. To remember or forget
where it resides or rises within us. More over that it simply
is us. Our choice of where we "place" that power
determines our space of freedom and the experience of the
life we have.

Truth
The most important note to take from this moment of
message is that you are power. The power of source is
you. There is no separation from it. All practice of
power is based on the fundamental truth that you are
powerful, because power resides as part of you. You
already are all you need to be. Only knowing, owning,
living and sharing your unique expression of it's spirit,
of the power that source becomes when manifested
physically through the vessel of your body brings it's
"power" to your life, moment to moment. Know it, own
it, live it and it becomes you. Share it and it becomes
our world as well.

With only my perception I can influence the experience of
my entire life. I can live in a self-created 6 by 6 cell, or
through the mirrors I bring into my life can truly cement
myself into ones of all shapes, sizes and dimensions. I can
come in and out of them based on the foggy haze I stay in.
Or I can fly high in the clarity of the moonlit sky I paint. The
choices are mine, based on the perceptions I have.

"I already am all I need to be" gives me the power to find
the freedom of flight, rather than the trapped bars of the 6
by 6 cells we all find ourselves in from time to time. Just
like the East Australian current we can ride it as it takes us
on the current of power, through the rise of spirit within us.
We might likely find ourselves in the same place in the end.
But the comfort and ease with which one rides the East
Australian current, vastly differs from the up stream paddle

another might find themselves in, as they dodge the jellyfish losing consciousness in their poisonous stings.

The choice is ours based on the perspective we have. I find the perspective we have greatly depends on where we stand.

That moment my father had his presence in places other than with me, a moment shaping many more to come. Was it him? Is he responsible for that moment? For the many moments that came after, moments shaped by the experience I had in that one tiny moment? Was it shaped by a consistency in a lack of presence over time? Is he responsible for that? If he is not, then who is? Is an eight year old?

Our lives take us through a series of events. Our choices shape those events, sure. And even at eight we are responsible. Maybe not always conscious of those responsibilities or the effects of the choices we are responsible for. None the less, they shape our lives. None the less, the choices are ours. The actions taken are done so by us. And the way in which we apply them, moment to moment, are of our volition; 8 or 88. With opportunity, comes responsibility; regardless of age. To be infinite, by its definition, power is blind to time, space, age and third-dimensional limitations. Thus are we.

A man the product of a rape. The rape of his mother by his grandmother's boy friend. By a man who "fathered" his son for only 6 short years. Until he walked out, looked his son square in the eyes and said you are now responsible for your mother and sister. A father he has yet to see again.

Another man a product of a father who beats his mother, neglecting him and his brother. A man who leaves his family, as well. Much less than 6 years after birth.

Both families left to poverty and pain. Two mothers left to find a strength that took much longer to acquire than the time it took their sons to age.

One son grows to be an incredibly responsible man with a solid character, a connection of spirit most pray for and a life most dream of. One son grows up with a rap sheet longer than the character of the other, an utter lack of self responsibility and an anger and rage that has ravished additional generations.

What's the difference? Moreover, at the core is there one? When both men lack the vision of the power of their soul, left judging themselves for the moments that are no more, leaving holes in their souls, where the power just keeps seemingly "seeping" out, is there a difference?

Does power have a face we see? Does it have a vibration we can hear, or result that indicates it? Is it something we know? Can I tell you all about it?

We each have crisis in our lives. We each have glory in our lives. We can all stand in the same moment and have entirely different experiences. It's called *crisis in perspective. And on the "other" end is Glory in perspective.* The point is the perspective of the situation. The power of that point lies in the choice we make because

---

Truth
And let me tell you the power is all your own. That includes its face, its voice, and more over the touch it has in your life. Power exists in every moment, whether or not. . . .

Your consciousness of its action in your life simply gives you the power to harness and focus it; taking an active role in crafting its results in your life.

---

of the perspective we have.

One could stand with my father and feel his presence. I did not. My children may stand with me and also be amiss my own presence. One could chant their voice and not know their song as I did in that moment.

I am asking you today to find your chant, your voice.

Your chant will move you. The vibration of it will shatter the life you knew. The light of it will blind those around you. The drunken stupper it will put you in feels like a hazy high, until the high is all you know and the flight is grounding regardless of what lies beneath your "feet".

So, I ask you to join me on this rather shifty journey as I share with you the various twists of my lens; the vision of my scope through the cycles of my power. May it give you the space to find your own scope, to ride your own waves consciously, in order to be the power that you already are.

All you need is your trusty little kaleidoscope. Yes run back into your childhood for a moment with me. Those little toys, that with only what exists within them, could change the perspective you saw through the scope over and over again. All it took was a little twist and turn. That's right, you didn't have to add anything, or remove anything. The scope already contained all it needed, to provide you beauty time and again. Just like you and I.

Yes, you already are all you need to be.

I spent 30 years, a marriage, two children, a few businesses, an accumulation of wealth, followed by a bankruptcy, a couple cities, a family, a grip of friends, a lot of tears, and even more laughter to get to a wisdom that I have always been, and currently am all I need to be, just as I am, right where I am.

I am a Woman. I am a mother, a daughter, a friend, a sister, and a granddaughter. I am a Woman. I am an entrepreneur, a business owner, a corporate professional, a writer, performer, speaker and artist. I am Human. I laugh, I cry, I scream and shout, I dance and sing, I have hope and fear, I have joy and pain. I am Human. I fall and stand tall, I speak and am silent. I move and can even sometimes be a bit still.

The kaleidoscope of my life shifts as quickly and easily as the turn of one. Shift, shift and the view is entirely different. It appears as if I am standing in a whole nother world with nothing more than a millimeter of movement. Shift, shift. . . the whirlwind of it all can leave me nauseous, and dizzy. The flight of it always leaves me lifted. The wisdom of it now leaves me grounded, even when I feel like I am flying.

When you look into a Kaleidoscope the wonder of it as a child is the ever shifting view we get by just shifting the end of the scope. The wisdom of it we seem to forget, as we lose our childhood "innocence" and gain our adult "intellect". You see with nothing more than the shift of the scope our entire experience can shift. We don't need to add anything, change anything or make anything more of the scope in our hands. We don't even need to know anything, learn anything or become anything to shift the scope. And no matter what the view is, our experience remains the same, wonder, after wonder of an ever-changing view that gives us the same inspiration time and again. Colorful and intricate, nonetheless. Beauty at each shift and turn.

Kind of like those dusks that set the sun each day, after day. Their beauty may shift based on the place you stand or the manner in which the elements in the sky have come together that day. But their wisdom remains the same. They are one of those moments. You get the chance to just dive right in and experience the divinity of truth. It's a dimensional opening where the light seeps through.

Just like the kaleidoscope, the dusk is just a shift of the light, an experience of an ever-shifting view that is beautiful because in truth it's always the same no matter the view of it we have. The peace I have, the passion I live and the power I am is found in the abundant gift of the Kaleidoscope. May you find the wisdom of her shifts in the shifts of your own life. May you rest in the truth that love resides in your heart and peace in your soul simply because you are. And if you wish for a different experience of the beauty that you are or the life that you lead, take a deep breath, stand still, listen intently and shift only the scope with which you are viewing and the entire experience will too.

Truth

The stories you read are from the scope with which I view them, the experience I had of them. Standing from a different vantage point like that of my ex-husband, my family of origin or my children, friends and associates, you might see an entirely different view. That's the beauty of the vessels in which we live. We get to see it through the eyes we were gifted with. And they are only given the periphery in which they are limited by.

Our wisdom, our souls though, are gifted with a vision that exceeds our eyes and minds. When we open ourselves up to the infinite possibilities of Truth we are able to experience all the abundance it has for us; feel the peace in its consistency, even when we know not the nature of its resonance.

Only when we lose judgment, slipping into truth are we able to garner the power of that moment.

Is my father a "bad" person or even "poor" father because I didn't feel his presence in that moment, or others? Probably not. Did my friends at the Tree House even know about, hear or experience that chant? Did they feel the soulful reverberation? Maybe. More important though is the power those moments had in shaping me. In each of them I get to decide what power I engage in them, what shape it takes in my life. Only my judgment of that moment, as well as those who are part of it, limits its power.

You see life wants us to live our power. Life wants us to grab "the bull by the horns" and run with it. It will keep showing up in front of us, our power that is, giving us chances through our choices to dive right in, to let it swallow us whole. Life reflects our own power back to us over and again each moment of our lives through the mirrors of people and circumstances that stand in front of us.

In each of those moments we get a choice. That choice always forms an action creating the result of our experience. Those experiences shape our perceptions that build our beliefs, becoming the foundation on which we stand. The foundation we base our next choice on. Without a consciousness of this process, those choices become results that we may think we had little to no power creating. However, in consciousness, they become the wand in the magic of our lives.

Remember, what we see and experience largely depends on where we stand. The foundation you stand on is built by you. Whether it lifts you up or has become a sink hole in the existence of your life, the power to shift is entirely yours as well. The power and tools you need to do so, exist entirely with you, right now; with who you are, right where you are at, with whom ever stands before you, and around you.

We get to build the platform we stand on, our life, through the choices we make in each moment. The actions that we take as a consequence of those choices build the place in which we stand, the life we live. The life we live, the experiences we have, shape the perspectives we take. And the cycle keeps on churning.

"On the road again! I just can't wait to get on the road again. . . " (Can't you just hear Willie Nelson?)

You've been led here to become conscious of your power. How it manifests, and often seeps in and out of your life. Knowing where you stand, how your choices got you there and how it can take you anywhere you wish to go, to be anyone you wish to be, opens up a world of power to you that provides a liberation no words may ever describe.

As you begin to walk through my path, its twists and turns, rises and falls. Know that these are my moments. Those who gifted me with their "character" and "script" had their own moments for their own purpose. Their path although it may have converged with my own, is entirely their own; as are their perspectives, beliefs, feelings and experiences. This is the scene of the path I walked as I came to know power, and live its glory.

May you also find the power that is your truth, as it is mine, in the scope you view your life with. May you live the power of your truth with a consciousness of the ability you have to shift your scope, of the infinite possibilities it has for you, and of the freedom you have to create the experience of them.

More Rabbit Holes

Shift, shift and down we go. . .

The Kaleidoscope has many shifts for us over the years. The process of finding our power is continuous.

And Round and Round we go in the shifts of the kaleidoscope we know as life. . . Shift. . . Shift. . .

At night, the sky would light up with stars that seemed to touch each other end to end. The grass was damp and the air almost musty. The strength of the ground holding me up brought a sense of security I craved.

I used to get lost in the grace of those stars. Those warm, moist summer nights softened only by the warm breeze still swaying in the trees. It brought me back home. To the home I only found within myself.

There is something to be said for Mother Earth and her ability to humble us. It's the grand points of her that bring us back to the little things, connecting us to all things. At least that's what it does for me.

Standing at the ocean's edge listening to her hum through the tides. . . Standing in a valley, staring up at mountains that seem to touch the sky with their finger-tips. . . Staring out into a field of corn that reaches into another field of wheat that stretches into another field of beans. . .The kind of fields that roll into the horizon where the sun sets beneath a sea of red and orange hues, tipped in pink, laced in yellow. Lying in the moist earth, tickled with her grass, gazing into her sparkling eyes that glow end to end in the stars above.

Ah, there is a point in all of us. A point where it all resides. What? You ask. What resides, where, you ask? It's a place I call home.

Some of us call home our houses that spread out over the land. They come with white picket fences and rickety ones as well. Some call home our cars. I have certainly done that a time or two. Some call home the streets that others drive on. Others are still wondering if home exists at all.

It does. Home exists. It resides inside of us. In that place we so often live without.

You see I know where it exists.

I know it because I tried to build it out there. I tried to build my home and raise my family in a house, with a white picket fence. I tried to park a car in the driveway that led to that house from the streets where others live. I tried to pay for it with a paycheck from a job I thought provided security. I paid taxes on that house to support the government I thought gave me freedom. I lived in that house with a man I called my husband thinking that marriage would provide me love, and family would secure its future.

When it all fell apart I learned the job didn't give me security, the government didn't give me freedom and the marriage didn't provide me any love. More importantly there was no other house I could go to that would give me the spirit I needed to get me through this!

That's when I found home within myself. That's when I began to understand what those stars had been telling me for 20+ years. That's when I realized the sparkle in those stars was my reflection. Those mountain-tops were the indications of the places I could reach, with my very own arms. That hum the ocean sang was my own song being echoed back to me. And the fields that stretched out into the horizon indicated the endless infinity of "space", reaching into those abundant sunsets. One sun sets. Another rises!

Lying beneath those stars at eight, feeling the security of the ground holding me tightly, I was searching for a power that would give me the love, security and freedom all humans naturally crave. They're as necessary as breath; love, security, freedom and joy that is. I now call them expressions of power.

We fight wars over it. We battle in politics over it. We lose marriages over it. We abuse children because of it. We judge others and criticize ourselves over it. We are starving, homeless, jobless, scarcity running rampant because of our search for it. Power that is. Our search for power leads us to war, abuse, and scarcity.

Somehow we got lost in the idea that we have to find it. Somehow we got lost in the idea that we don't already have it. Somehow we got lost in the idea that it is anywhere we are not. Somehow we got duped into believing that it's a search, a journey.

Somehow we missed that we *are* the power. Somehow we missed that we simply need to reveal it. We simply need to honor and live the power we already are.

Power isn't something that is gained from those outside elements. The house, the government, the job, the church; they can't give us something that is us. That may flip the world-view for a few of you. If so, get ready to stand it on its end!

The house is just wood.

The government is just a system.
The churches, and their religions, are just structures.
Marriage is just an institution.
Spirituality is just a word.

The only power that exists is the power you have
within your very own body rising as spirit in the temple
of you. It's the very energy of the life you live. The
love you crave loves you right now. The freedom you
desire presently frees you. The security you need
keeps you safe in this moment. Break the bars, open
the box in your chest, and feel the ground beneath
your feet!

The power you long for is the breath you take, the skin
you live in, the eyes you see through and the ears you
hear with. It is you my friend, given life by the spirit
that rises in the temple of you. The search is over. All
you need to do is see the reflection in the stars, hear
the echo in the ocean and feel the sky at your finger-
tips.

It can't be that simple you say. . . . . right?!

We humans try to make things so complicated. It
really is that simple.

Beauty is: it doesn't need to be created, found or
taken back. Authentic power already exists within
you. In fact the only place it exists IS within you.
More over, if the only power that exists is the power
you have within yourself, there is enough power for us
all. You see, when I connect to my power and you
connect to yours, we no longer have a need to fight
each other for the power we found within ourselves!

Power now creates peace. The world-view is now flipped on its side. And the world out there, now gleans from the inside out.

{For those who are religious or spiritual. Please note I didn't remove God, Spirit, Love or what ever you call it. I just shifted "where" "it" is at and in what relation it is to you. And if you're still confused do the following two things. First go back to your "bible" or spiritual material and read. . . "made in the Image of God". Second, hold on for just a second and stay open to a truth that might present its self in "time" if you let what might not make sense to you now, show you its truth in a moment.}

My world needed to be flipped upside down, literally, in order for me to get this point, as you have well read thus far. It certainly is more than just a point of power, but a powerful point none the less.

It could have been the point I was praying for my life at the forearm of a drug-crazed lunatic that once called himself my loving husband. This was a powerful point to experience. To experience how powerful external factors can be in altering the power of the self altogether that is.

It could have been the point I was thumbing through the yellow pages searching for programs my taxes had supported for so many years in those thousand dollar paychecks. You know, those programs that were suppose to pick up those who had fallen and give them a lift back to their feet. It was certainly a powerful point to realize I had to sell everything I had earned, and leave the home I had in order to get assistance in keeping one. In order to get the funds to buy back everything I had just sold to qualify for the assistance that would no longer be enough to give me a lift back to my feet!

It may have been that night I sat up sobbing, wondering how I would have enough time and love to raise two small boys on my own. Then again which night was that? There is power in knowing there were so many of those. Even more power in knowing now how cleansing they were.

It might have been the night I raced down the freeway at 3am thinking that if I just put enough force into it I could shift the situation and get back that sense of sanity, that house on the hill, and the family dinners at 6pm. It was even more powerful to realize they didn't really exist in the first place.

Maybe it was years ago. That night I got a call from a friend, telling me that two more had passed into another dimension over night. And the one I got only months later that still another friend had moved into the light beyond here within 6 months of diagnosis. And we were not even 20. There is great power in recognizing the power of the moments we are gifted.

More likely it was the moments over time.

Whatever the point was. My life flipped. Whether it was the tears or the reality, probably a little of both. My perspective blurred and another one appeared. One sun set. Another rose.

Shift. . . Shift. . .

And that's about as simple as it seems today. One sun sets. Another rises in the morning. There's a point in our life. Whether it comes in a bang or smolders over time. We all come to a point where our power emerges.

It doesn't get handed to us by the government, or found in a church. It isn't written in books like this one or told to us by our parents. Power doesn't come in the form of a house, a paycheck, a bank account, fancy clothes or titles. It doesn't even come in the form of accolades, or accreditation. Even though I am one of many who paid over $40,000 for pieces of paper that will tell you I am accredited by some of the most accredited universities in the world. [Did you ever wonder who determines who accredits who and what it really means?]

I could walk you through my trophy hall showing you how many people and places value and regard my results! In the end, my power is not shown in the trophies in my hall or the certificates on my wall. My power is shown in how I honor myself. My power is shown in how I service it to others in the shadow of it all.

Our power is revealed in the moments we claim it. It lives in each of us in every moment we breathe. It doesn't always require our life to be flipped upside down, or over on it's side for us to see and more aptly feel the power we hold inside. However, sometimes it happens that way too.

Once our life is flipped inside out, in whatever manner is necessary for us, powerful living can emerge.

Power is not perfection, and size does not matter. Living powerfully does not mean one is perfect, nor grand, just that they own who they are, are responsible for themselves and take action in their life.

I may not be perfect. My life may not be grand. I falter at times. I cry often. I laugh more. I get angry and I play too. Sometimes I can pay my bills. Yet, I am always abundant and prosperous.

Not much different than the times I fought for my life, or raced down the freeway. Not much different than the nights I cried myself to sleep at 8, or 28. Not much different than the last time I thumbed through those yellow pages, or took the hard calls that life sometimes rings.

And at the same time, very different. The moments don't change. We do. Powerful living infuses our lives with a different tone. A different feel.

My ex-husband still "haunts" me. It's the nightmare that won't end, and the love that will always be there. Friends still come and go, in life and death. My bills still get delivered with an eerie timeliness. They still need to get paid with that same timeliness.

Consequences still evade every decision I make. However, I now claim my responsibility in them. The action I take is not through my words, but with my movement. The movement is generally a flow, rather than a force.

I have surrendered to the truth that life is a flow and how I flow in it determines how much water gets in my boat. I can either sink or sail of my own volition. It's now liberating to know the wind in my sails is my very own breath. I just need to take it in and then let it go. Take it in and then let it go.

Shift. . . Shift. . .

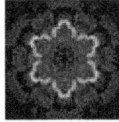

Ah, the webs we weave. I used to play little 45's on my red and white striped record player when I was a little girl. I would dance and sing to a powerful little song. "It's a small world after all. It's a small world after all. It's a small world after all. It's a small, small world!"

I would sit on this rickety old fence my grandfather built, my father repaired and my brother was working on as I sat there. I gazed out over a field that met another field on its right and yet another on its left. The highway, in front of that field I sat gazing out at, only broke briefly the connection to another string of fields on the other side.

I was only eight. Yet I sat there pondering how the children in Africa could have an average death rate around my age! How could there be so many little people like me sleeping in streets busier than the highway passing my house? How could they be so hungry when we grew so much corn here?

I sat in that small town in the middle of America contemplating the world's scarcity that seemed so far away from that fence, the corn fields and the fidgeting feeling I had inside.

Today I realize new depth in the message on that 45. It is a small world. We are all weaved together. Small town America, big city New York, bustling Beijing, and stifling hot Egypt share the human experience. From Russia to Paris, Sydney to Toronto, people live the human experience. And our kaleidoscope keeps on turning.

Shift. . . Shift. . .

We all fight in search of love. Does that make sense? To my eight year old mind that made no sense at all. To my 28 year-old mind it still made no sense at all. Today that remains the same.

The questions I asked then. I still ask today.

Why can't we all just love each other? We can. Why can't we all just have what we need? We can. Why can't we all live in joy, laugh and play? We can.

Innocent? Maybe. Alive? Definitely. Idealistic. I hope!

It's as simple as seeing a reflection in the mirror others provide us. It is as simple as knowing that we are in ourselves what we see in others.

It may be scary to look at all that anger. It may be frightening to feel the hatred shining back at you. It may be terrifying to see the fear in their eyes. It may be alarming to notice all that judgment and criticism. I hope it is. It just may shock you right back into yourself! Oops, there you are!

Shift. . . Shift. . .

While playing those 45's on my record player I would dance around my toy room in the basement. There are so many tools a little person has to learn about the

world. I would hold my favorite toys and take myself
away from that small rural town and into my dreams of
a big, bright, world alive with possibility. Back then I
only needed to look into that tiny hole in my cardboard
kaleidoscope. Shift, shift and away I went.

Today I only need to look out into the world in front of
me to see that same kaleidoscope of possibilities in
the web of connections we form together in this small,
small world. A powerful perspective provides a big,
bright world alive with possibility. It's our
kaleidoscope, our big people toy. Shift, shift and
away we go!

The Scope of My Lens

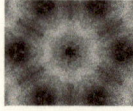

It was a bit breezy, as it always is on the ocean. The sun was beginning to set on the horizon, which didn't bring about the extra warmth I craved. And the moisture in the air was engulfing my skin. It felt like the dew must feel on the petals of my roses on a spring morning; damp and cold, yet soft and comforting. One deep breath in of that moist, clear air was warming however cool it was. I just took it in; breath, after breath.

There were two other boats sailing in the distance and the coastline was barely visible behind me. I laid my head back on the blanket spread out over the bow. The pillow behind me lifted my head ever so slightly and yet as soft as it was allowed me to fold into the feathers. I took one last look at the setting sun before I closed my eyes saying goodbye to the day.

This is my favorite time of the day no matter where I am. Dusk that is. When the sun is half down, and then just on the other side of the horizon. Maybe it's just the romantic in me that loves Mother Earth's natural dim switch. The red hues, she often blesses us with in these moments of the day, seem to sing their own song. The night has yet to fall, though you can feel the depth of it approaching. The lightness of the day is waning, and yet you can still feel the inspiration of its light. Ah the romance in it. . .

Then again, more than the romance, I love the message dusk provides. It's the moment of the day when we are gifted the opportunity of reflection and foresight, all at once. The silence of it fills me even when I pay it no attention.   Gratefulness absorbs me.

There are many moments in life that just allow you a direct opening into truth. Dusk is one of those moments. You get the chance to just dive right in and experience the divinity of truth.   It's a dimensional opening where the light seeps through.

You see, dusk represents the integration and cyclical nature of life it's self. Standing in the silence of dusk gives us the opportunity to see the loss of time and experience the presence of life. The day is finished and tomorrow has yet to arrive. Time eludes us and silence sits in its presence.

Some people may ask "Where is that, if it is not "here? When is it, if time has escaped? How is it, if there is no Way? Who is it, if there is no man? What is it, if there is no box?"   The answer is in the dusk of the days we live.

The mist now began to spray my face ever so gently as the waves crashed against the fiberglass with force. The boat began to rock with the waves of the night that were creeping up faster and faster. I continued to take breath, after slow breath.

My eyes were startled open by a large crashing noise. I leapt to my feet, now firmly planted on the earth below me. I took a minute to get my bearings. The energy rushing to my head made me a little light headed. And this light was so much harsher on my eyes now open. I took a quick stretch and another deep breath. As I could tell, it was gonna be necessary.

The banging was getting a bit more erratic. He always tried to be so quiet, as if I was not aware of his arrival. The energy of the house reeked of it. The time of night clearly communicated it. Four am, it was sure not to be my mother-in-law. The boys were fast asleep and my reverence for animals living in their natural habitat, rather than mine, left me sure it wasn't the clattering of any pets I missed.

I peered out at the moon, taking a deep breath, prepping for what only God knew was really arriving. I could hear all the closet doors opening, a bit of clambering around inside and then they closed as fast as they were opened. Furniture was being moved tonight indicating a rather viscous suspicion had arrived. All the lights were now on and the stairs were articulating the timing of arrival.

Of course there were 4 rooms to the left, that were yet unchecked. Since the episode was commonplace, timing was still clear. A bit quieter now though, as if the previous noise was not enough to wake them, and some bit of reverence had arrived amongst the demons. I sat still. Focusing my attention on my breath. Relaxing my body parts one at a time.

As the lights dimmed behind him, and the doors closed, I knew there was one, critical place left; the room in which I resided. It was filled with three closets, a bathroom and a window to the roof. Yes the roof! As if the house wasn't clear enough. The roof was a possibility.

You see that's how paranoia works. It has no reason. It has no connection to truth. It dove off the other end of "reality". Both ends are just as maddening in my opinion, paranoia and 'reality' that is.

Although this was *my* experience of it, let's be clear, we all experience varying levels of fear, paranoia and the numerous other names we refer to it as. Sometimes we call it reality. Other times we call it paranoia. Let me tell you if it isn't truth it isn't there. Reality might as well be paranoia at that point.

Sure my husband at the time was an extreme experience of illusion at work. But illusion is still illusion no matter the form it takes. Two story houses, white picket fences, kids, partners, titles, spotlights, credentials, friends, ribbons and bows, even smiles on our faces are no different than the ice he blew when they are devoid of the authenticity found in truth. From the housewife to the banker, from the man on the street to the woman on stage, shielding the truth is shielding the truth.

"Where is he!?" He shouted. "I know he's here!"

That's right, another deep breath. Eyes now closed again. I took deep breath, after deep breath, focusing on my center while the swarming continued to blow around me.

Watching a living death is much worse than witnessing physical death eating someone away.

My uncle died of chronic emphezima. Now there's a sight. A 70-year-old man wilting away, covered in brown spots, unable to even take the very breath of life that makes earth a reality to us. Two grandparents, a college friend, and family friend after family friend has been eaten away by cancer in all its various forms. From two months to two years, it has its own schedule, taking one organ after another until there's nothing left to function. There's of course the horrid site of AIDS, and the quick death of "accident". There are those who died of internal hemorrhaging that appeared to be fine. Yet the blood, and the life, just seeped right out of them.

Yes death isn't always pretty. But to watch someone take breath after breath and not have an ounce of life in them is another sight altogether.

There is nothing more painful than watching the death of a man standing in front of you with the gift of life wrapped in a red bow in front of him. Watching him kick it as if it would pop open. Then sit back and watch, as if it would open on its own.

He had the lungs to breath and gasped for air. He had the heart to love and felt only sorrow. He had the mind to know, the eyes to see, and yet he was still climbing on the roof to find whoever had to be there.

Truth
It's all the same state just manifested in a different reality. It's like water, truth that is. When you put ice cubes in a glass of water and they melt. Will the water over flow, be reduced or stay the same? It will stay the same. H_2O is still H_2O whether or not it is ice, liquid or gas.

Fear is still fear no matter the manifestation it takes or the intensity with which it is expressed. It will still create the same result. Fear is still fear when you melt it down, or evaporate it into the air. The truth is the truth when you melt it down, or evaporate it into the air.

In fact, when water is evaporated into the air do we lose more water on the earth? It just causes precipitation and rains back onto the earth. When it falls to the earth again and rains into the ocean, does the ocean over flow its edges? The ocean has no edges. Neither does truth.

Yes he blew ice. Yes he was, in that moment, a paranoid psychophrenic experiencing a manic episode of bi-polar mixed tendencies infused with 30 years of rooted rage. He may have been high, just as likely coming down, or feening for the next fix for that matter.

He pounced back in through the window. A bit more frazzled than when he began. Finding nothing to validate his fear only added fuel to the fire that had been burning long before he got home, and originated deep within. I was practicing the same surrender I am today, asking myself what reflection this was mirroring for me.

Yes that's right if you are looking at it. It's a reflection. If you are surrounded by it, you are it. Fear is fear is fear, death is death, no matter the face you put on it or diagnosis you give it. I guarantee watching it happen to someone breathing regularly, with blood flowing powerfully and no diagnosis of 2, 6 or 9 months yet to go only means the timeline has yet to be communicated.

Was he the life I married or the death standing before me? Was he the mind diagnosed insane, or the spirit I so loved? Was he the body being eaten away, or the soul I felt everyday?

Where was the truth I so longed for? Must it be in the reflection in the mirror?

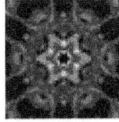

I stood in the mirror the next morning as the kids were showering for school and he laid passed out cold. A mirror so big it ran wall-to-wall, counter to ceiling. With a mirrored cabinet to the right and one hanging on the left, there was no running now.

Yes life had me in a corner. It was stand there staring at the death before me, or stand in the truth that shattered the mirrors before me.

I was taken back to that pain in my chest. Where did it come from? I could trace it back as far as I could recall. That little girl rushed to the emergency room time after time with pains no one could find, that the soul within were screaming with.

I labeled that sorrow within as a desire to save the world. I spoke words of being the first female president. I saw visions of for-profit homeless shelters infusing the world with the self-responsibility necessary to sustain anything handed out. I achieved diplomas of social service in order to serve in the Peace Corps. At home or abroad I was determined to save, save, save. I would wipe the tears of the world and soak up the sorrow I knew in my heart was not my own.

With my Birkenstocks on and flag of savior held high I dove into the social service of America. You gotta love the system. When I felt bruised, battered and disillusioned by the truth - that the system I was part of kept them in the very life I intended to save them from - I went running again.

I landed square in the middle of the Dot Com revolution. The age of information we called it. Ah ha, I thought. I have found the lost souls ambitious enough to do the work. I found those souls who searched out abundance. Until I realized *doing* isn't *being* and a desire of abundance doesn't mean a mentality of such.

Those in glass houses shouldn't throw stones right!? So I went home to save my family, my husband, our life. Until he fell off the bed and still didn't wake from the drunken, high-infested coma he was in. Only then did I have to get out of bed and look in the mirror as I brushed my teeth to start my day.

Standing in front of that mirror I wondered. How did a well educated, strong, self confident corporate woman raised with such great values end up in a 2-story house, with 2.5 kids, and a rose garden that doubled as my white picket fence in the land they call paradise by the pacific? Filled with this reality inside that look a lot more like the families I had spent so many years "saving"!? Why was I looking in the mirror at the women I answered the phones for and counseled in groups?

In a last ditch effort to escape the mirror I went back to bed. When I laid on my right side I could see out the big bay window over-looking a lush, nature-filled hill. The blue birds sang and the hummingbirds hummed, while the family of rabbits played. It was my country paradise in the middle of a bustling city.

I swore I was in my home, but the windows looked a lot more like the bars on the jail I just picked him up from. Although I lived blocks from the ocean, the pillow was beginning to feel like I was drowning in it. I could smell the salt from the sea moisture in the air but the salt I tasted on my tongue came from the ducts in my eyes.

Now it was me gasping for air as I realized I was the one dying all along. I was the one that couldn't catch my breath and the flow that had stopped was in the veins pulsing in the skin I called home.

Standing in front of that mirror, the eyes I have seen through my entire life were now looking right back at me. No matter where we are the eyes will always speak the truth. Truth is funny like that. It always seems to find us in a mirror.

We can run, but we cannot hide. Euphemism? Or Fact?

The truth will find its way to us. From the eyes of my ex-husband to the eyes staring back at me in the mirror, the truth was gonna find me. If we choose not to listen to the ones looking back at us in the mirror, life will bring the mirror to us; one way or another.

My ex-husband mirrored my own inner fear. My own inner lack of truthful living. Sure my words were honest. My commitment was solid. I said what I meant and did what I said. I was passive, peaceful rather than violent and attackful. Although, what is violence, rage and anger, but fear at the core. Is it really integrity when you're not living your own truth? Maybe our fear and lack of integrity manifested in different masks, but the eyes behind those masks remained the same.

Since I wasn't gonna look at the truth in my own eyes. The world found eyes that I would look into. And those eyes brought me the truth, like it or not, one way or another! It simultaneously brought me right back to the mirrors in my own bathroom, with a chance to look into my own eyes.

That morning, as I looked into my own eyes, I was given a chance, a chance to see my truth. I saw it.

The light always shined through like rays of sunshine on a very dark morning. It just shined through these very thick bars.

Shift. . . Shift. . .

Laying there, holding my breath without much
knowledge of doing so I focused on the burning in my
diaphragm. I couldn't feel my skin. I could, however,
feel the blood running through my body. It's all that
gave me the knowledge that I was even there. I
could smell the stench of his sweat as it dripped onto
my body.

I couldn't move if I wanted to, and not because he was
holding me down, but because I had left my body
altogether. And yet I was all too present. I knew he
was watching the tears as they ran down my face, and
yet there was complete silence from my mouth. I just
stared up at the ceiling knowing it would be over soon.

The ripping of my heart was acute compared to the
tearing of my vagina.

The burning sensation of one melded into the
smoldering of the other. His lips touched my breasts
and the shrills that ran through my nerves couldn't rip
me far enough away. The breath I suspended
couldn't make even the life inside of me end.

And in an instant the water poured over my face,
running down my bruised body. I couldn't curl up tight
enough. My nails couldn't scrape the elements of him
off my skin quick enough. With my breath still
suspended, the tears just kept falling. Not even the
heat of the shower could evaporate the stench. The
burning persisted and the blood kept flowing down the
drain cleansing out the semen he left behind.

Although my bruises were not on my skin and my back alley was lit with the lights I had purchased myself. I had to remind myself what we all do. That nothing was hurt that could not heal its self.

Rape is simply a violation of another; to force submission upon another, taking from them in order to fill ourselves. If we can't see how we are doing it to ourselves, raping ourselves that is, life will bring it to us!

Some of us get raped like this. Some of us rape ourselves. Some of us get raped at the bank, in a job, in a relationship, a contract, a back alley and our very own homes.

I have been raped in my own bedroom, in a barn full of hay, in corporate America and public domains. The details may vary but the essence remains the same. The truth of them all remain at the heart of slavery its self.

Slavery is not just about the socio-political suppression of a people. It is ultimately about consciousness. I had become a slave. I had lost sight of my truth. And since I wasn't gonna look at the truth in my own eyes. The world brought it to me again in eyes I couldn't deny.

You see, liberation evades us in moments of unconscious living where our truth is hidden in the smoke we put in our pipes of denial. The only truth that exists is the one we see with our eyes open, and the one that remains when we close them.

Power is the convergence of the two. When what we see with our eyes open remains the same when we close them we know we are seeing the truth. When what you feel in your hands matches what you see with your eyes closed you know you're living the truth!

What I see with my eyes is discerned with my mind and felt by my heart, and manifests in my hands.

Which remains the same with my eye's both open and closed?

Go back to that story of what appeared to be me being raped. Now close your eyes. Imagine the feeling of those bruises throbbing on your skin, the stench of his smell. Taste the salt from the tears pouring down your face and the burning in your vagina, or penis. Imagine the blood running down your legs as the hot shower you are standing in washes it down the drain. Even the steam can't evaporate your pain and the fetal position doesn't tuck you far enough away from the memory.

The truth is now the pain you feel in your heart as you imagine with your eyes closed the rape you appear to be hearing, and now experiencing in your imagination. The truth is the aching you feel in your bones, the breath you've suspended and the tension in your own nerves right now.

The power is in the connection you feel to the truth of that experience. Whether or not you have been sexually raped you can feel the pain when your eyes are closed or open. It's the only truth in that story. What you read with your eyes and discerned to be one thing in your mind, only the truth of your heart knows. It's a story of pain.

The truth of it for you can only be found by looking into your eyes in the mirror staring back at you.

We rape ourselves everyday with the validation we give to differences our eyes may see and our minds discern. The only truth that exists is the one in our hearts. That has no color, or size. Hearts all speak the same language, do the same task and have the same purpose. They literally feed life to our bodies with the blood they pump.

Still standing in front of the bathroom mirror. With memory, after painful memory, flashing like a horror movie on the big screen of my life I just gasped for air. The air I had been suffocating out of my body by denying my truth. By living the expectations of others. By doing what I thought I "should" do. By doing what I needed to do in order to avoid judgment, avoid persecution.

Being burned at the stake was no longer a metaphor or past life experience. The flames rose high fogging the mirror in front of me. I could hear the crowd chanting. Burn her! Burn her!

Oh no!! The truth was fading from sight. I could barely see my eyes in the mirror in front of me. It was now or never. The memories of pain, the human faculty to protect, were rising in those flames. I reached forward to wipe away the foggy mirror in a last ditch effort to keep the truth alive. I gasped again to see the match that lit the fire in one hand and in the other a bucket full of water to put it out.

The match had been lit by me! Although, this time the power to squelch that fire lay in my hands as well.

Nelson Mandela inspired world peace from a literal six by six cell in Southern Africa. The leader and founder of the Crypts gang, inspired world peace, from a literal six by six cell that began as one in his mind forged by the one he lived on the streets.

Our upper middle class white homes are no different than those six by six cells when we relinquish ourselves by standing still to the "fears" created in our minds. The one often delivered to us by "others"; the media, the *Wall Street Journal*, education, experience, statistics, business, spreadsheets. The reflections we created. They are all masks to the ego of fear within us that limits the power we have within. Making anything possible! The bricks we laid to build our cells are whatever method we choose to use, as our excuse for standing still.

I could stand behind the thick bars in front of me. Or I could put out the fire and the illusions of slavery all at once. The truth is found in the liberation Nelson Mandela and the founder of the Crips realized in their six by six cells. Truth, and the liberation it provides, is available to us all as readily as the bars that bind us, Nelson Mandela and anyone else; from the suburbs to the hood, from the cells to the blocks. We choose them, liberation or slavery, through our personal action and reclamation of truth.

Reclamation of our truth is not easy. Simple maybe. Easy, not always. Reclamation of truth, through the process of acceptance, can be painful when the realization that floods the fire burning is that of self-responsibility. Freedom comes when we balance that acceptance with the reality that everything leads us back to love. Herein lays forgiveness. What follows is freedom.

Acceptance of self-responsibility may cause what feels like third-degree burns in that fire. The forgiveness given when we accept the purpose provided, that everything leads us to love no matter the path, heals. The wounds that may have been third-degree burns become silky skin.

Standing in front of that mirror as the fog of denial cleared, if even for a moment, something that would prove to be just as challenging was left. If I had led myself into that fire, I had also carried the logs, prepped the brush and lit the match! I was responsible for the truth of my situation now. And with each moment being the only moment there was. I was responsible for each of them, as much as the next.

Instead of lifting the weight, I felt 500 pounds had been added. What happened to truth freeing me?? As soon as I grabbed hold, the flicker of freedom had just as quickly dissipated. Truth is as much a process as it is a "reality" or fact. It is fluid. There is only the moment and that moment is dynamic. As soon as you attempt to hold it, it will elude you.

Blame gives us the illusion of lightening our load. However, in that moment accepting the truth surely felt much heavier. I wasn't sure which was illusion and which was truth. With my human eyes I saw so much judgment, the "wrongs" I had done to bring me to this mirror. The mirror I had brought myself to. How could such an educated, spiritually evolved woman coaching others, have done something so atrocious to herself!?? To those around her in the process??

There is a natural process we humans take ourselves through called guilt. It's our process of preserving the persecution we know so well. Self-persecution that ironically "comforts" us. Guilt is the 500-pound weight we feel. Blame is its illusory counterpart delivering the goods. Giving us the chimera that we can eliminate the heavy feeling. It's another choice we have, to slip back into denial and out of truth.

Blame appears easier. It seems like it would lift the load that's weighing us down. However, until we feel that weight and it's combined desire to be lifted, do we have the simultaneous opportunity to stay in truth and BE light. Remember how we determine truth. Truth exists in what remains with your eyes both closed and open.

When you blame, and then close your eyes, that weight still exists. When you claim, instead of blame, you become light when your eyes are open and closed. Yes, you actually have to carry that load, and accept that you piled it on your own back. Which means you have to figure out where you got it from and put it back, in order to lighten the load.

Truth just is what it is. (Explain a game where you have to undo it the way you did it.)

Acceptance is what I now faced. That meant accepting all of me, which includes what appeared at the moment to be wrong turns, detours and all out crashes.

Truth
There is no place you are that you are not meant to be. Often stated as, "The Grace of God will never lead you where the Will of God cannot hold you." That includes what appears to be "wrong". There is no right or wrong. There is no good or bad. For some of you this may be a very radical concept. For others it may conjure up a feeling of, "Duh, I know that. That was in the 101 class!"

Let me tell you knowing it and living it are two very different things. The practice of a knowing is what creates results. If you are still reading this book, practice it. Radical truth requires radical acceptance. Truth is total and thus requires our acceptance to be total as well.

It means every moment is meant to be. It takes acceptance of the fact that nothing but love exists. Nothing! That includes our choices, our actions, our relationships, our "consequences". Everything, I mean everything.

Even what appeared to be "evil" or sinful, dark or jaded, on the part of my ex-husband was simply a reflection of my own inner fear covering my truth. It was also the path that led me to the blossoming beauty of truth that eluded the fear. Acceptance, in practice, loves the "pain" as I did the laughter. Feeling the peace of the truth I arrived at only through that seeming horror.

Truth

Not everything is what it appears. Beauty, love and joy can come in the most unforeseen places.

"Every morning, the water carrier of Stanislav would walk from the well at the edge of town through the same shtetl streets, toting his two buckets of water to his customers. Day in and day out, he performed his routine with a simple joy.

One day he was particularly joyous and burst out in song along the way. But his song was interrupted by the sound of weeping from one of his buckets. The bucket called up to him, "How can you sing so joyously? Are you blind? Don't you realize what a bum bucket you've got in your hand? Don't you realize that for years now I've been leaking? Look at your other bucket – he doesn't leak! I don't know why you didn't use me for kindling a long time ago. What good is a bucket that leaks?

The water carrier gently responded to his bucket, "No, my bucket, you are the one who is blind. What good is a bucket that leaks, you ask. Well, look and see.

With these words, the water carrier made a grand motion toward the ground beneath the bucket, pointing out the same path they had walked for years. Look, my leaking bucket, look at your side of the path – the yellow daisies, the wild red strawberries, the luscious greens. Now look at the other side of the path, the ground beneath my sturdy, leakless bucket – it is nothing but gravel and dirt. All of this beauty is precisely because of your leak. For years now you have watered this side of the path, making it the most beautiful thoroughfare of Stansilav. Your leak is what makes me sing!"

Grafni, Marc Soul Prints. New York: Fireside, Simon and Schuster, 2001

Now I may not have had to travel down "this" path. It was a choice I made. Other choices were available, certainly. Now, I choose to see through my own eyes, rather than into another's to see my truth. Either way, though, the experiences brought me back to the truth always alive in me. It placed me in front of that mirror so I could see the eyes I had been longing for.

The point is in the purpose, rather than the process. The process is our choice.

So why did I marry a man I knew was a coke addict.
Why did I marry a man I knew I did not want to spend
the rest of my life with before the plans began? Why
did I forgo all the intelligence I paid for with time,
sweat and dollars?

The power of judgment, another face of fear. I masked
it as commitment, and responsibility. It even reared its
ugly head as expectation as often as the rest. But it
was really judgment.

It got mailed to my home seal with shoulds. That's
right you should do this, you should be that, you
should have all this. They came with these pretty
collectible stamps on them and stickers on the back
where they were sealed so tight. But they were still
shoulds. Judgments no matter how pretty they looked
or fancy they were packaged. Expectations that were
so tightly laced they were choking the life right out of
me.

You are "supposed" to get married, take the name of
another in order to be tied together. You are
"supposed" to have children in marriage, right? You
are "supposed" to raise them in a family, right? The
Disney family, your family, my family, what the hell is
family? You need to be supported by another income,
right? Your word is your deed. You're "supposed" to
stick to your commitments. It's called integrity, right?
You're "supposed" to solidify love with a piece of
paper, right? You're "supposed" to build a house
together. It's called a home, right? Stability is found

in those four walls we call a house, protected by the white picket fence and infused with joy from those little crying infants, right? I am "supposed" to grow up and be an adult, which means we "should" mortgage everything, right?

Sounds kind of funny to read now. I also know it's not the words that read humorous to me as much as the experience of it. Oh how we bind ourselves to silly little limitations, illusions that wreak as much havoc on our bodies and lives as that ice he blew! That's right, what's in your pipe? What are you smoking? What fear are you breathing?

Not all fear is smoked into your lungs through a pipe laced with crystal meth. But let me tell you the death it provides is all the same. The burning sensation as it goes in and the hacking as it comes out is all the same. The black smoke it creates and the one it surrounds you with is all the same. Fear is fear whether or not it's smoked in a pipe.

Judgment is judgment no matter the face we place on it or the plate we serve it on. If we are being anything other than who we are right now in this very moment we are smoking a pipe laced with judgment. It will kill you all the same.

It took longer than standing in front of that mirror that tired morning to accept all that truth. With lungs black from years of self-judgment, acceptance of it from others, expectation that swarmed around it all and the second-hand smoke delivered from others, a clearing out had to begin.

We humans feel so compelled to judge. Judge even when we often think or even feel that we are loving, doing "good" or "righteous" things! Take the tree huggers, the eco-activists, the women of NOW – the National Organization for Women - and the Anti Defamation League. So righteous they are to point out how wrong the "other" is.

They are doing great things, right?!

If I learned nothing but this, by breathing that second-hand smoke, ironically labeled ICE, it was that judgment comes in many packages. Even the one wrapped in my very own body. With all my "righteous" acts I was still standing in front of a man so full of fear. If I was so tightly laced to him through marriage and family, there was fear in my very own soul being reflected back at me. That I am sure of.

Thus lies the same truth for those so enflamed with passion for a "cause". Let me school you for a minute. My lens that is. . . . [Smiles]

There is no cause but the truth of you. That's right. You. If I am selling anything it is You. I am selling you on you. If there is a cause to be found in this book, I so rebelled against writing, it's the hope that you find your own story revealed in the mirror reflections of mine, those mentioned here and the ones standing next to you in your very own stories being lived in your living rooms, bed rooms and board rooms.

The tree huggers, the feminists, the communists, and those fighting the cause of democracy all have an irony self built into their "causes". The common theme of judgment and hate. Even if your cause is to rid the bad and right the wrong you are engaged in hate and judgment. Whatever you're engaged in you're sure to be delivered. A war on crime, a war on hunger, a war on violence; what do you think all of those wars deliver?

That may light a fire of rage in some of you. Maybe you are calling it righteousness if the denial is thick enough. Feel the trigger? Feel that anger inside of you?

If you are out to be right about anything, someone has to be wrong. If you have a cause or a "Way", it is to say there actually is a "Way". Rather than simply knowing there is only truth, the kind that exists eyes open or closed, expressed through so many beautiful souls, languages and stories.

If you are out to save something, something has to be less than its divine truth and beauty in order to be saved. You may be able to mask it in a brightly painted face, with red and pink colored hearts, carry white flags and badges of honor. The hate still exists.

To save something it has to be less than whole, and thus not the truth. And that's just not the truth, now is it?!

Are chemical plants, oil spills and natural human neglect and consumption destroying the earth? Maybe. Are animals, children and even you and I being abused? Maybe. Is there racism, anger and rage from culture to culture, race to race? Maybe. Is there sexism, ageism, and a million other-isms? Maybe.

Maybe the truth is that it's all the same thing. Maybe it exists in each of us. Maybe it's actually an opportunity, or opening for us to love more deeply.

Let's flip the perspective on its end for a minute. Let's twist the kaleidoscope and see what we see. Let's seek out the truth. Let's look at it through a few stories.

Gary Zukav gives the best analogy of intention I have ever heard. "If you put milk into a glass what are you going to drink? Milk. If you put water into a glass what are you going to drink? Water." You will get out of your glasses that which you put into it.

So many of us are fighting a cause and don't even realize why the fight keeps raging. "Why can't we just cure the illness in our world? Why with all this effort, intention and action is discrimination still running rampant?" We ask.

I went to a NOW convention in Las Vegas. I was a bit inspired by the passion I found in these women. They ranged in ages from 17 to 75. Some had strong recollections of the civil rights movement. Others were part of a whole new movement. All of them grappling with their own identities on the search for it in their cause, what to call it, what action to take.

They had conversations about language, bringing in the young women as part of "the movement", reenergizing women in the world for "the cause", how to bring in activists that felt alienated, how to partner with others on a similar mission. All of it revolved around the same theme. I am not sure they were even conscious of the significance it had on their very own discussion of such. Separation.

They themselves were fighting a cause of separation. With a desire to merge the chasm they felt so large between men and women, and in this age of the movement, separation amongst humanity. I guess if they have arrived at the awareness it's about humanity and not just women they are moving toward it. However, they still missed that the very fact they see separation, validates its existence.

Truth

Something doesn't have to exist unless we see it. We create our very own realities. Yes, what you see is what you create. And vice versa, you create what you see.

Have you ever sat in a conversation with a group of friends and then each re-described what has just been said? Did you notice that each of you described the same situation and conversation very differently? In some cases you each heard a very different story, heard different words being used even.

Have you ever noticed that two people could watch a situation and remember or see different details? One individual may notice very little, while another notices vast details. One may remember a green hat, while another saw it as a black hat.

According to a study done by Patricia Tollestrup, John Turtle, and John Yille, and written about in *The Accuracy of Eye Witness Testimony,* both bystanders and the victims picked the accurate criminal only 48% of the time.

This is the power of the mind to create its own realities. When we are aware of how our minds work to create what we see around us we can begin to touch the very iceberg of what we can create with a trained mind. We can begin to see how we can manifest the world we live in. How we can actually shape the physical world in which we experience.

http://ezinearticles.com/?The-Accuracy-of-Eye-Witness-Testimony-and-Its-Flaws&id=328261

It's like war. Do we ever heal a world by bombing it?
Do we eliminate fighting, by adding our own righteous
armor to it? Those women were poised to fight the
fight! They were going to fight the government, the
right wing, and anyone else they could find who stood
in angst of their cause.

What are they putting in their glasses? A Fight! What
do they see? Separation! [What you think you
create!] They hate discrimination so much they were
going to pitch a flag and fight for their cause. Thus
adding hate to their glasses masked as deep passion
and vision. Ironically creating more of the very
separation they wished to eradicate.

Gotta love the irony!

I went to a big fancy dinner for the Anti-defamation
League. It's a cause started after the Holocaust to rid
the world of hate, hate crimes and more discrimination
ensuing for Jews and now others; another cause that
has broadened its horizons to include hate against all
people today.

A vastly published author, well spoken and highly
acclaimed man spoke at the dinner honoring a local
woman. He was passionate. He had high volumes of
energy swirling inside of me. I thought, "Yeah! This
guy is fired up!" Until, again, I realized. He hates
hate! He really hates hate! Another cause pouring
hate into their glass, and this time to end hate its self.

Can you rid the world of hate by hating it? Can you
bring peace to the world while judging another? When
you state or claim a cause you are inevitably stating

that there is someone else that you are not for, a thought, a philosophy, a cause, a belief, whatever it is. You have to judge them for what they are in order to ever have a reason to build a cause in the first place. To be right, one must be wrong. That brings judgment to the plate every single time!

Causes, thus, are inevitably flawed. It's like a cat chasing its own tail. Back to the mirror we go until we can see the hate raging in our very own eyes. Pouring more and more hate into the bucket. Churning and churning it until we get so tired and frustrated we throw in the spoon landing on our knees. Until we throw our arms up and ask "Why? Why God?"

Mad and frustrated we ask, "Why all this madness, God?" And we wonder why we get laughter in return. [Laughs] "How can you laugh at a time like this?" We ask! "People are dying, children getting sold, women getting beaten; our environment is getting eaten literally." Mad, mad we are. And we ask, "Why so much madness in the world!?"

If you are not laughing, take a minute to read that last paragraph one more time. We drink that which we pour into our very own glasses.

Staring into that mirror of horror I found the hate, the judgment and the anger in my very own eyes. Do you see your own yet?

Judgment. Judgment. Judgment.

Not all judgment happens in action. Whether it is
direct hate, or the mask of it, through a cause against
it. Listen to this one. . .

Less than 500 people populate this town. Yet the line
hardly says so. You could wait for over an hour, in
lines that swing around the corner of this rickety old
town block. And that was in the winter months. It may
take up to two hours on a breezy summer Wednesday
evening when the college kids are back.

All this for a side of chicken so greasy they placed it
on bread to soak up the residue. Served pickles with
the plate of crunchies in order to soak up the oil left in
your mouth. They waited hours to eat off paper
plates. Forks upon request as if you were in a sushi
bistro. High heels were especially dangerous on
floors so slippery the waitresses tread with caution.

We ordered in line and took our seats. The young
waitress came to take our drink orders. My friend
looked right at her and asked for a Pepsi and that fork
that comes upon request only. She looked him dead
in the eye and past him by asking me what I'd like. I
thought she must have impeccable manners to ask
the lady first. She then moved to my friend on the
right and on around the table. However, she never
made it back to my friend on the left.

Assuming she got his first request I left it alone.
However, I could sense his uneasiness. I leaned
over and reassured him she heard his request. He
just looked at me with these eyes filled with a cross
section of sadness, disappointment and intense
discomfort.

She appeared back with our drinks shortly. She
placed them in front of us and began walking away.
As she turned to leave I said, "Miss, you must have
forgotten his Pepsi and fork." She looked at him with
this look of her own discomfort and said I'll be right
back, as if it was a trouble to serve him.

I took a deep breath and apologized. Not really sure if
it was my place, but clear he was there because he
cared enough to see where I grew up, experience
places that were special to me.

This was not the first dinnertime experience of racism
I had. I am sure my grandfather found it rather
appalling that a 7 year old would disrespect his
authority so much as to tell him he had no idea about
the world if he believed there were differences in
people based on anything, especially their skin color.
My parents dismissed it as naivety at such a young
age.

As a teen my father found it widely acceptable to have
"colored friends". However, any intimate
interconnectedness was just beyond unacceptable.
Though, is it love, or friendship, when there are
limitations on the manner, way or depth with which we
show it, live it, share it?

Truth

Love is limitless.

Limits are created by the human being. They are constructs we develop in order to create order, safety and stability. Or really, the illusion of such, that gives us the feeling or sense of what we believe it is; safety, stability and order. Because our minds have yet to be trained on how to manage the chaos that it receives, it attempts to order it through constructs and boundaries.

Boundaries can be very valuable entities. However, when they are extreme they become limitations. There is a fine line to walk in balancing boundaries that have no limitations. Boundaries are valuable and effective when they are built with malleability.

It's like the construction of a bridge. Every engineer understands the need for a bridge to have sway built-in. Have you ever stood on a bridge and felt it sway with the wind? That was part of the design. The bridge needs to be able to sway with the natural flow of the wind in order to maintain its strength.

Its strength comes not from the rigidity you may think it requires, but from the actual built-in sway and malleability of the structure. It's another wondrous example of how what appears to be strong in the steel is actually strong through is pliability.

> Love is like this. It's limitless. That means that love
> has no conditions. It possesses total acceptance.
> That includes the moments of what may appear or
> feel to be harmful, "wrong", sinful even. Love's
> strength comes in its pliability.
>
> Love happens not when you have discerned the
> truth as you define it, or when enough time has
> passed, or experience has been had. It is instant,
> total and all accepting.
>
> Love is a truth. Thus is doesn't understand
> constructs like time, limitations, expectations. If
> they exist, it's only because we created them.

My rather "accepting" mother found it acceptable to
tout a belief in my perspective, she said. However,
she argued, we live in a world where the children of
such a connection will have a very hard time in the
society with which we live. It's just not a good idea
she would say.

"But I am not racist," they both claimed. What
appears to be inaction is just as much a choice of
action, as the visual movement of action.

I thought I had experienced hate at this point.
However, I learned the extend of my naivety did not
truly come from the misunderstanding my grandfather
thought I had, but the one I had of the very nature of
hate it's self.

Anytime love is "absent", fear is present. Standing still
in our two-story homes in suburban America is still
judgment. Sitting at my grandfather's dinner table and
choosing silence is fear. My father masking his fear in

"friendship" with all its limitations is still fear. My mother masking her fear in limited acceptance, but "acceptance" nonetheless is still fear. Are you feeling your own fear yet?

And don't get me wrong taking up a cause is not the action of love. Anything short of love is only fear. That's all there is love and fear. We can call it hate, anger, rage, war, a cause, passion, or pretty faces like acceptance with caveats, and friendship with limitations. We can even say we love because we do not hate. We are passive. If you are standing still, if your arms are close to your body, your boat tied up at shore, you are short of love. Just because fear appears to be absent, doesn't mean love is present.

Truth
Love isn't a journey. It's who we all are. It's existence.

My mother, my father and grandfather, NOW, the Anti-defamation League, the Democrats, Republicans and communists; they are all spreading love. Even in judgment. Their perspective of it.

Sometimes the only eyes we're willing, or able, to look at are those of pain, anger and hate. Even the eyes of my ex-husband poured the deepest well of love into my soul. Had I been able or ready to look through the eyes of joy they'd have appeared. Even hate, anger, judgment and fear speak love in all their varied languages.

Irony is, if we all knew and lived the truth - that we're all love, all "perfect" just as we are – I bet we'd all spend less time saving the world, ending hate in others seeded by ourselves reflecting back to us the apple we ate ourselves. Celebration and joy are choices we get to experience when we choose to shift our perspective to one of love, rather than judgment.

The lessons remain the same. How we get to experience them is our choice. Joy or Pain? Happiness or Anger? You are free to choose. You built those bars. You have the key to free who you are. Free yourself.

Love is action! Being is also an action. Anything dynamic, anything alive, is action.

Shift, shift. . . .

Now you remember everything is love. Even the judgment that "they" are not in love is judgment. See the paradox. Round and round we go until we realize we are. Breathe in and out, in and out. . .

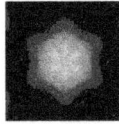

By the time this morning had arrived my husband had been to at least five in-house rehabilitation programs. He had been in NA and AA, both court ordered and self-chosen. Well, self-chosen is a bit of a stretch. He had really chosen to attend because he wished to please someone. His wife, his mother, his friends, whoever was campaigning sobriety to him at the time, or required it as part of their love connection in his life. So he often "chose" it himself in order to maintain the relationships he desired.

But addiction, both his, and my own I found in his reflection, is a truth we must come to on our own. The face of one of my own addictions displays this best of all I think. When a woman is living a life of domestic violence it is very difficult to position yourself in any way that will encourage her out of it. Denial is so thick in this form of addiction that the very light of it can push her deeper into the addiction.

In domestic violence one is so wrought with their own guilt. Surviving on the threads of denial. It's the best indicator of a personal truth missing. She is so void of her own personal truth that she must deny even the truth of the "reality" in which she is living. Any hint of it coming to the surface, being called out by those around her, asking her to face the truth, and she will push it deeper within.

This is manifested in her lack of sharing what happens in the home. Fewer calls home or to friends. Makeup on the scars, and bruises. Sure we may believe that this happens because he won't allow her to call, or forces her in. The truth is she needs the denial. It's all her own! She created the walls around herself, even if she manifested him to build them.

Now I know this is a radical shift in perspective for most of us. This means that she is not a victim, but a cultivator of the violence it's self. Some of you may say, "This is a dangerous perspective to take. It continues to beat the woman who is beaten."

Let me assure you from a woman who has been beaten, she beats herself more than any of you, or any man could ever do himself. The pain of those bruises is a welcome deflection of the emotional pain that cuts deeper inside than the butcher knife he scrapes across her face.

Making her a victim just adds to the bruises allowing her to sharply shift the addiction. And by the way, calling her a "survivor" is just a shift in terminology. The addiction isn't actually shifted. Healing only occurs when we accept the truth of our own "realities".

 "Hit me, Hit me!" I screamed. Standing at the edge of my desk in my home office I was screaming louder than he. With the phone in his right hand, I shouted, "Get it over with. Do what you want to do. Come on, hit me!" There was so much anger inside of me.

Sure anger at him for yelling, abusing, for controlling and antagonizing. I could say it was about the lies, the terror, the stalking. And yes, it wore all of those masks. But the beating that was happening was happening by me. He just mirrored my inner anger back to me.

I was angry for being there. I was angry for not being able to control the situation. I was angry for even being alive. I was just plain angry. With *Imagine* posters hung on the wall behind him and the unauthored poem *Attitude* hung to the right of him I stood there screaming, "hit me you bastard, hit me!"

I spoke about love. I wrote newsletters on the power of belief to my corporate clients, and trained executives on positive attitudes. Yet here I was, wishing he would just hit me. I knew the pain of that fist would smash the real pain right out of me. The focus would have to turn to the bleeding nose or the throbbing cheekbones. At that moment even I was fully conscious of the insanity.

Still, I screamed on until the phone hit one wall, I landed on the other and he hit the door headed out of the room. The emotional pain throbbing inside of me brought more anger that there was no physical pain to move me out of it. Curled into a little ball, tears rolling down my face, screaming still!!

At that moment I became clearly conscious of the fact that I wanted him to kick the shit out of me just so I could remove the focus on the throbbing inner pain that was melting my life away. Anything, anything to move the focus off of me.

So let me tell you, conscious or not, those women built those walls themselves. They may not have landed those punches, but they created them on their own faces. It's not about fault, theirs or his. It's about

truth. Yes, if we stay in the world of fault, in which we've lived, saying, "It's her fault" we may cause more "damage". Crazy as it sounds though, I am asking you to lift yourself out of the reality in which you have created and drop yourself right in the middle of the **truth**!

There is no fault. There is no right or wrong. There is no good or bad. There is only truth.

When you can drop the right and wrong, the blame and fault, there is no challenge accepting the responsibility she has for herself. Truth is just the truth.

A woman (or man, child, etc.) living a life of domestic violence shatters the truth whenever it approaches her. She shatters is it even when it comes in the form of aide pulling her out of that dark well she lives in. Whether or not she knows it she keeps those walls around herself. She brought that abuser in and she keeps him in. Denial is her friend!

She is there because she fears love the most. She doesn't want to feel pain. Her own equation of love is that of pain. And the pain he puts to her face is much better than the one she feels in her heart, the one that resided there long before he knocked on her door. Denial is her only protector. Denial of her personal truth and most of all denial that she is in the situation she's in, or that she herself put her there.

Yes the light of that truth brings more pain than savior. From the outside looking in, anything to give her the chance to pack her bags and run to Timbuktu, we think, is a savior. It comes as a shock that this "help" is often met with anger, and more denial from her, shot at the one who delivered it. Why would she not take the hand stretched out to her?

Every addiction is like this. That of food, sex, drugs, love, dependency, abuse you name it. It all breaks down to denial of personal truth. They'd like to run so far from their truth, the one that feels so painful; they'll do anything to get away from it. Even if that means finding a physical pain that hurts worse than the inner pain. One that deflects the one we want to deny more than the one we created.

Take a woman in the throws of bulimia. She vomits up the truth she can't hold inside of her. Every time she puts the nourishment of life inside of her she can feel it growing. She can feel the life growing. The life she lives to deny. The truth she cannot live with. Simple as that.

The anorexic starves the body in order to deny its existence in the first place. To put nourishment in the body means there is actually a life that is present in the first place. Anything else is a story we've made up, a blame we've placed, a judgment we've landed. Denial takes on many forms, appearing with several masks. Denial is our veil to the truth.

Yes, that woman needs her denial. The one that she is not in an abusive home. Just like the denial that delivered her to that abusive home in order to deny the pain inside of her in the first place. If you unveil the one of her situation. She must unveil the one of her truth! Thus you get to experience the wrath of her anger you thought only existed against her in order to save her from what you thought was outside of her.

Women in domestically violent homes display this as clearly as any other. But all addictions have this at their core. They need to protect their truth. Keep it hidden way deep down inside. And because it only lives within them you cannot deliver them from it. Even though you think pulling her from that home will save her, only she can deliver herself from hell, back to the Garden of Eden.

No matter how many times I drove that man to rehab, he would always come out the other door no less than five days later. Delivering him to the front door did not mean delivery. Delivery does not come through any front door made of wood, steel or iron; even that of the ones we think we find it through on Sunday mornings.

Delivery is found through the doors of 'love'. Those doors only exist in our very own hearts in a direct connection to the source. We may see a vision of it on Sunday mornings. We may get a taste of it in the intention we get delivered on the front door step with. Even those are not the truth. Our truth that is.

Our truth is our living.

My husband was not going to get delivered by a man preaching on Sunday, anymore than he was with me doing it daily in our home. He wasn't gonna get delivered by the words in a book or the trainings in a rehabilitation room.

Racism isn't eliminated by my father having colored friends, nor does love live in my mother's heart because she doesn't hate other races. Judgment lives when we do not love. Even the lack of hateful action doesn't mean we love. Even the "highest" of intentions doesn't bring love to a situation.

Judging my husband's addiction and harping on his choices was not creating an abundance of love. Telling him he was wrong. Making him feel shameful and less than he was by telling him all he "could be", was not loving him for the truth of what he IS.

Lying on that pillow drowning in my own tears of terror I felt nauseous. I had so much yellow-bellied fear living in me and the truth of it could no longer be denied! My body wanted to vomit the entirety of it right out. Literal projectile came thrusting out of my body. Life's metaphorical "reality" came crashing in again. Laced with all the drama my life had ensued to this point!

I was just like those women in NOW and that man speaking at the Anti-defamation League. I harbored the similar reality my grandfather did at the dinner table, my parents did in their belief constructs and murderers, terrorists and out right racists did. I was the husband I so loathed, the addict I drove to rehab and the abuser I blamed for the bruises I was crying over. I was living fear, my fear.

My eyes throbbed and my stomach contracted over and over again. Dry heaving now. Trying to find all the remnants of this shit that just hung in my being. I curled up trying to stop the pain in my stomach. More over trying to protect the only way my body knew how, by curling up so no one could get it.

The only way to find love is to be love. Sounds so much simpler than the action of it requires. It's easier to fight the fight of the flaming cause that someone is hurt and I am gonna ride in on a white horse in all my brilliant regalia, dressed in silver armor and carry them to safety.

I met this beautiful man one night. His eyes were piercing and yet graceful all at once. He had this ability to hold you tight with just enough space to be free at the same time. He was tender and loving and yet you knew he could protect you against the worst of the worst in a moment's notice. You know, the kind that has his eye on everything not out of ego's sake, but out of pure awareness. The kind that allows even the most independent woman to let her guarded sense fall into his arms for a moment because everything else is covered for the minute.

He was intelligent and funny. I laughed like a little girl. We danced for hours, being playful enough to lose sense of the crowded club around us. He was capable of having clever conversation with a connection of spirit, and emotional availability that sang in chorus of one another.

So I asked, "How does a beautiful 34 year old man like you find himself single?" He said it was because most people could not handle his profession. "And that is?" I asked, thinking "here is the "but" to all his beauty." He said "I kill terrorists. I am training to be a Navy Seal."

"So you kill people for a living!" I said.

"What are you passionate about though?" I asked.

He said "taking out the "bad guys", killing the terrorists. It breaks my heart to know that people live with fear. From terrorists to the people they meet on the street. There is no greater pain than walking down a street passing a white man in the dark of the night and see the terror in his eyes because I am a black man. It breaks my heart to see any kind of fear in another's eyes."

I rephrased my question. "So are you passionate about taking out the bad guys or making sure people feel safe?" This light went on in his eyes. "How did you know that? My true passion is making sure people feel safe!"

Sometimes we get lost in the idea or picture we've created of our truth. Kind of like this man of beauty. He rode in on a white horse, built himself like a chiseled out quarter horse with muscle definition to die for. He was dressed in brilliance and doused in armor. Yet clouded by the very steel in front of him.

Again, you cannot save someone when there is nothing to save. Let's go back for a second to that woman living in a violent home. You cannot deliver her from something she is not in. She may appear to have bruises caused by a man striking her. You may be able to take her out of that home. You may be able to get her to a safe house, find her a job and give her the tools to begin "rebuilding" her life.

If the foundation on which the first house was built is not torn down, the walls of the new architecture may look different. The base will still be the same. We can save our Illusions. The truth doesn't need saved. The truth is the truth. We simply need to reveal it.

If that man is saving a world from a terror that is only an illusion he is a cat chasing its own tail. He can work as hard as he chooses. He can chisel that body, and learn to hold his breath for long periods of time to run missions in the night approaching from the sea.

He is approaching a phantom enemy, even if it
appears in flesh.

Fighting a terror that is self-created by "humanity" only
validates a terror in the very people he wishes to feel
safe! The fact that he is fighting a terror tells them
there is something to be fearful of. The armor he
wears communicates to them that there is a need for
armor in the first place!

Are there bombs being dropped in our world? Are
people dying at the hands of others? Are there people
spreading terror in the world around us? The more
important question is. . . .

Is our terror any different than theirs? Whether it's
masked in radical right winged protection or Muslim
extremism it is still fear. It's still a need to hold so tight
to a belief construct that protects a "reality" we think
we need. The irony is, it's all an illusion anyhow.

In order to be love, that chiseled out soldier riding on a
white horse into what appears to be a battle of epic
proportions actually needs to lay down his armor right
there. Right there in the middle of gunfire shelling its
way toward him. He needs to lay down his armor.
Strip out of his regalia. He must stand tall, with no
white horse to hold him high. He needs to stand
naked with arms wide open in order to find the radical
truth of love in the middle of an illusion so thick with
gunpowder his vision has disappeared.

That's the beauty. Love is all around us. Love is in
every situation, every person, every land we fight. No
matter the mask they wear. Be it a mask of out right
fear or the one of a cause. Be it a mask of love in all

its truth and glory. All that lives when we close our eyes is that of love or fear. The choice of which to embrace is wholly ours. And by the time you get to truth you'll find out even fear is an illusion. The only difference is the experience of the journey, of our living.

Yes, it appears so simple. Yes, the radical action of it feels at first so incredibly difficult. However, there is comfort in the truth that irony can be as much a friend, as it appears a foe. Irony is even ironic to it's self.

Standing there projectile vomiting the reality I had created in order to make room for the truth meant I had to love the man vomiting next to me. The one sweating out of every pore, the chemicals that had been turned into a dingy yellowish white powder, packed, rocked and then crushed in order to smoke in his glass pipe. The stench was as bad as the truth I was facing.

I had to love him for all that he was right there. I had to love him for all of his choices. I had to accept that he was making the choices that were best for him in that very moment. Everything is love.

At this point let me tell you there are no regrets in life. Just opportunities. My husband was the biggest opportunity with the best gift anyone could ever give me. Aside from the meshed DNA found in our sons and the love we will share that is far beyond this time and dimension, I got life.

Some of us just have to stop breathing before we can feel the power of the breath we take. They've always called me the Queen. Now I understand the power of the Drama in it, and how my son came by it naturally! Love lies in everything, no matter the face you put on it, the lens with which you view it from, or the experience you have of it. Truth is just truth. And life gives you moment after moment to breathe it in. To experience it.

Truth
We don't actually become anything, although that may be the only words we have to describe what it feels like. We already are all we "need" to be. We are what we are. Truth is truth. That applies to the truth of us as well.

That's the realization. Who we are right now, exactly as we are, in each moment is the truth, our truth. All we are is love. All that exists is truth, which is love. Everything is love, including my then husband exactly as he was then and is now. That's right. A crack smoking, psychophrenic, angry, abusive man,

---

who still isn't the father I might like him to be or his sons crave him to be, is still all love. My experience of his love was, and still is, a reflection of me. And the story is only my experience from the lens of my scope. Even our belief that love is not real, or that what you just read is incorrect, is an inkling leading us to love.

When you experience love windows crack wide open, the lids are shattered off boxes and doors open. When you live love walls aren't real, doors aren't necessary, boxes don't exist. Every experience until then simply gives us an opportunity to experience love. To taste it, be in it. Filling us with the longing to know in our truth. To remove all that covers our truth. To own and live our truth. To be, thus, share the love we are.

The point, again, is in the purpose. The process is the choice. The gift in every moment is love, whether or not we choose to experience it.

Marriage to my then husband was a life of love, lived through an experience of fear, standing in the illusion I created. It led me to my truth. This time I choose to claim the gift of the love in the experience. My cycle began to shift. And the power I had for so long shifted to others began to shift back to me.

Just like every other experience I had in life. From the jealousy found in competition in corporate America, to the expectation I experienced in my family of origin. From the abuse I experienced, to the love I shared with friends and lovers along the way. They were all experiences of love. The vision I saw in them were only the reflections of my own inner fear shading the truth.

I call them points of power. They're found in the moments, moments like dusk. They are openings to the truth that is. In every moment there is an opportunity to open the gift of ourselves. To experience all the love we are. Just like that box, wrapped in a red bow that my husband still kicks in a fleeting attempt to open, still stands staring at, wondering when it will open it's self for him.

There is little I can say that will explain what it is like to love. The truth is just the truth. Human words limit love every time they attempt to explain it. Even experience is minute for what love is, for what you are.

Yes, it may be radical. The idea of loosing everything you learned in order to remember all that you already know! Getting lost in order to be found. Finding our universality, our connection, in the individuality of ourselves. Something as radical as the truth, of love, requires action as radical.

Remember even radical is a bit human in nature and thus not all that different than illusion. So caution. . . .

In order to love you must speak love, act love, know love, choose, be love. Everything around you must encapsulate love or it is not love. What you think you create is a truth more powerful than I could ever explain in a book, or otherwise for that matter. Truth, as I have stated, is something we must come to ourselves.

An experience for me may not be the same for you, and vice versa. The perspective you have in the moment is only for you, and with one small shift of the lens you shift its perspective. The moment you are in becomes a new moment. Regardless, what always remains the same in those moments is the truth that is; eyes open or closed, moment to moment.

Radical is only as radical as your current limitations. Why don't you step into the dusk with me?

Stand at dusk with me and witness the opening beyond this place we understand as time and space. To a "place" where time does not exist and space has no edge. Where cyclical gives new meaning to infinity.

Come to where love is all there is. Where acceptance is all that's practiced. Where surrender is so natural it's not even found in the dictionary. Where the joy in me is the joy in you.

Take a deep breath in. . . . .And out. . . .

It's a bit breezy, as it always is on the ocean. The sun is beginning to set on the horizon, which doesn't bring about the extra warmth needed. And the moisture in the air is engulfing our skin. It feels like the dew must feel on the petals of the roses on a spring morning; damp and cold, yet soft and comforting. One deep breath in of that moist, clear air is warming however cool it is. Take it in; breath, after breath.

There are two other boats sailing in the distance and the coastline is barely visible behind us. Lay your head back on the blanket spread out over the bow. The pillow behind us lifts our heads ever so slightly and yet as soft as it is allows us to fold into the feathers. Take one last look at the setting sun before we close our eyes.

It's dusk. When the sun is half down, and then just on
the other side of the horizon. The red hues seem to
sing their own song. The night has yet to fall, though
you can feel the depth of it approaching. The
lightness of the day is waning, and yet you can still
feel the inspiration of its light. . . . .

Feel the comfort in the warm breeze. The freedom of
the wide-open ocean. The connection of others on
the sea and friends lying next to each other. . . .

Take deep breath, after deep breath. . . .

If it's in me then it's in you.

When I stood in my truth, I stood in our truth. Truth is
truth. It is for me, as it is for you. If I am love,
everything around me is love, leading me to love.
Then you are love too.

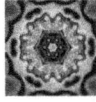

As I finished the vomiting and pulled myself together I jumped in the shower. The day needed to begin. My then husband was certainly passed out and by the nature of the previous evening I was certain it would be for at least the rest of the day. Plus the boys were beginning to wake and the joy had entered into the room in the presence of their little angelic bodies, smiling faces and big hugs.

As I emerged from the shower, they hopped in. We all got dressed, fed and prepped for the day. It was almost Christmas time. So we headed out to complete our last minute shopping. It was refreshing to join the space of the living, with all those people bustling around during the holiday of joy. We finished our shopping and headed back.

As we arrived home, he was still passed out as I had suspected. Considering it was dinner time, and my family was gathering at my sister-in-law's home about an hour away, I decided to pack the boys and head up north. It would keep us all away from the drama that was sure to ensue once he awoke and clambered through his recovery mood swings.

Not to mention, it was time for me to regroup and determine the course of action necessary to live the truth I came face-face with that morning. Clarity is undeniable when you have swallowed the pill of consciousness. You can still deny it if you choose, but you now have to look it square in the eye as you do!

Surrender is all you can do at this point. A good friend of mine always says, "All you need to do is say 'yes'. God will work out the details!" Acceptance is the first step in surrendering. So I began there.

However, for someone who doesn't know the practice of acceptance it's a lot easier said than done. Sure I knew what acceptance was. I even knew some exercises to apply it. Again, I was not shy of education, information or the library of research in my own personal library. However, I was lacking experience. And again, the point in creating results is the experience gained in practice.

So how does one accept when the only way to truly BE it is to practice something you've never been? To do something that makes sense only to your mental faculties. You see what most books explain as acceptance is just another practice of mental masturbation. Yes, that's right. Stroking your mind in order for it to feel relieved.

True acceptance is a revelation that in practice is much different than anyone can explain in words. There are no words to describe the vastness of it's gift and the practice of it's requests. In fact, our natural human tendencies of self-preservation make authentic, total and whole acceptance quite a challenging practice.

Stand outside. Take your shoes and socks off. Place your hands outstretched fully on either side of you like our logo. Tilt your head up to the sky. Close your eyes. Take in a deep breath in both your diaphragm and stomach. Breath out letting go of all that is inside of you.

Now pick up a bowl. And tell me what you come with.
What do you come to life with?

Tell me what you'd like to place in that bowl, or take
back with you.

Here's the irony. . . .
If you came with anything in your bowl or are
searching to place anything within it, you are outside
of yourself. You are in expectation, and missing
acceptance.

Now take that bowl and throw it away. Throw away all
that you brought in it and all that you wanted to place
in it.

Stand outside again. Take your shoes and socks off.
Place your hands outstretched fully on either side of
you like our logo. Tilt your head up to the sky. Close
your eyes. Take in a deep breath in both your
diaphragm and stomach. Breath out letting go of all
that is inside of you.

Now stand there. Stand still. Feel all that runs
through your veins. Feel the nerves on your skin.
Feel the light pulsing, the breath flowing.

When you are in life. When you are living. You, are
what you bring. You, are what you experience. You,
are what you bring back with you. Each time you
breathe in you accept into you the life you were gifted.

Walk into the next interview you have.
Walk into the next conversation you have.
Walk into the next relationship you start.
Walk into the next negotiation you make.

Walk into the next moment of your life.

With your arms stretched outward. Your head tilted upward. Your chest open and exposed.

Say 'yes'.

Accept. Accept all that is available. Accept all that you know. Accept all that you know is possible, all that you have no concept of. Acceptance is experience. Acceptance is more than win/win. Win/win is still a mental manipulation of our ego's desire to gain. Acceptance is being the energy the ocean was created out of, instead of swimming in it, fishing from it or even being the ocean it's self.

So throw out the bowl. Stand with your feet grounded in the dirt below them. Stretch your arms out, tilt your head back, breathe in and expose YOU! Let the tides roll in and out, in and out. Whether or not its high tide or low tide, the ocean is still full. It's still flowing. It's still the ocean. You can either be the life that created the ocean or bring a bowl to it.

Your choice. . .

You see. Acceptance is a powerful tool when you dive right into the liberation of truth!

It's exactly what my friend was telling me. All you have to do is say 'yes'. The details will work themselves out. Acceptance is coming to the plate whole, with absolutely no concern, expectation or desire of what, how, when or where.

Just say 'yes'.

Startled by the loud, and rather constant by now, ringing of my cell phone I finally rose from my long anticipated slumber and looked at the caller ID. Sure enough it was my home number! It had been a day and a half since I had left for my sister-in-laws. Now I am no math major and it's the only class I ever failed in my life. Calculus and I just never got along! But, yes the math adds up. That was almost three days of being passed out cold.

By the third consecutive call I picked up the phone. Holding the phone about half a foot from my ear I waited the typical 3-5 minutes for the screaming to end. My mother-in-law lying next to me just looked at me with these eyes of understanding that took her years back to the generational experience before me. I think the fear that this was her own blood, combined with the flash backs she herself was having sent her into a bit of shock.

As he calmed enough to listen to where we were I explained we were at his sister's house and that we had been here for almost two days now. Of course, the paranoia was still ever present. Not that it was ever absent. Even the offer of speaking to his mother lying next to me didn't calm his racing mind, and delusional fantasies. Threat upon threat just kept getting thicker until I could hear nothing but glass shattering all over the room he had scoured floor to ceiling only three days prior.

With the speakerphone on so his family could hear the entire episode, their nerves began to get rattled a little as well. You see, denial runs deep and is generally threaded in strands called DNA. Addiction is very good at veiling it's self in shrouds of secrecy. That are of course upheld and further complicated by the co-dependant. I was the master at that and starred quite well in the episode without even a script to read from.

As she sat there convincing me to call the police, making sure we didn't arrive back at that house without an escort, that would further escort him, she had only her grandchildren and our safety in mind. Although, that may have put their father in jail again, it kept us out of a grave. That was confirmed by the death threats he made on my life to the police who entered our home via the garage, ambushing him in that bed he hadn't arisen from in 3 days. The threats continued as he screamed through the double glass windows of the cop car on his way past us sitting one block down the street.

Acceptance doesn't always present it's self in the easiest manner. Coming from a very traditional family, Christmas was a big day and my second favorite holiday of the year. For so long I had held on to things because the timing was never right! Yes that's right, back to those expectations and judgments.

I mean what is a family if it has only one parent? What is Christmas if the father and husband spends it behind bars? Or anywhere but setting out the milk and cookies, playing Santa all night and waking at 5am to those pitter pattering feet?

That's right, I withstood all of that for the simple hold I had on an illusion created by the judgment and expectation that family needed to be a certain thing. Holidays had to look a certain way. I should provide for my children in the same manner as my own family had. I completely disregarded the truth of our personal existence and the realities of uniqueness.

It was time for acceptance. It was time to clean up the shards of glass, and shattered mirrors of illusions. It was time to put up a new mirror, patch the walls and throw out the glass. Nothing really lives in those glass display cases anyway! Nothing of real value that is. If it breaks upon falling it's more than likely not the truth.

I spent the rest of the week patching the rather large holes on three of the four walls in that master bedroom. I rehung the mirrors and threw out all the glass. For that matter I threw out most of what was in that room. I pitched every sheet, blanket, pillow and symbol of my fear that was left standing in that room. A symbol of my own in the process of purging all that I was now revolting.

Acceptance meant wholly or not at all! It meant night, after night of red puffy eyes in the mornings that followed. It meant that Mrs. Claus took the place of Santa this year. Not like that was a new occurrence. But this year she was on her own. No red-nosed reindeer to guide her.

I simply needed to stand in the truth no matter what it brought, what it looked like, and especially what it felt like. It wasn't always pretty. It certainly wasn't always easy. And every day was not exact. It's not a science, it's a practice!

By now I had certainly accepted the truth of addiction, both mine and his. I knew it to be the truth way deep in my bones. I understood in my being what it meant and how it lived in our lives. My veil of denial had lifted that chilly Christmas season so many years ago.

Standing in line, about 6am, it was still freezing. Even for Southern California. I wrapped the blanket tighter around him and coaxed him to finish the bottle knowing we couldn't take it with us. In front of me was obviously an extended family, a man of about 65, a woman about 48 and a youngster about 11. Ahead of them was a woman wrapping her arms around herself to keep warm. Behind me there were about three toddlers playing together.

Children have no boundaries and judgments about the people surrounding them. Spread a smile and let out a giggle, share a toy and you're in like Flynn! Their mothers made small talk about what brought them to this line. The conversation always varied vastly from the women in line at the grocery store. And the line extended man, after woman, after child and grandparent for about a block and a half. Some speaking their native language. Others not speaking at all. Still others, like those little toddlers, making friends with the faces they shared not only this space with, but their toys with weekend after weekend.

Every face has a story. And the story is rarely revealed by the face. You could create your very own sitcom right there. Rarely would you be accurate.

Creative maybe. Just the shared dialogues and unshared innuendoes were enough to create a classic 30-minute comedy/drama combo. Considering I lived one of the real life stories behind the faces, I can tell you drama it was, comedy it could be! Of course what you see all depends on where you stand. Shift. . . Shift. . .

A mirage of epics right there in line, one after the other. Not all of them very clear on what the real story really even is. "It's his first offense," was the common monologue. Easily after that were the monologues; "It's not a violent crime. It's only a DUI, petty theft, and/or drugs." How can you see the truth in their faces when they didn't even know the truth themselves?

All wearing iridescent veils cloaking our truth, protecting our "realities". The same faces showed up week after week. It began to be a make-shift support system, a sudo-family of sorts. Often not even words were exchanged. Matched eyes and a shift of the lips to a half grin was enough to share the support and understanding that even though we were there, all would be fine.

Women have an easy way to share an experience at a depth unknown to most men. [Or maybe that's just because I am a woman.] I never told her how I felt, but she knew. As I picked up the bottle and handed it back to her, as another opened the door for the stroller I was pushing. I watched yet another share 'Cheetos' with a little one screaming at the height of his impatience for a very long wait. We all showed our support, our acceptance in ways we didn't need to speak.

Everyone shared the commonality of their rich denials, their undying love of the one who betrayed themselves worst of all. They all stood there for hours waiting to see the one behind bars. To sit in this caged in "park". Complete with benches, picnic tables and vending machines. The kids ran around playing, beginning to believe and understand that all the daddies stood in line, with their hands behind their backs until the guards let them into the park. All the daddies were in 'time out'. That's what my oldest son grew up knowing. Most of the women in their immediate surroundings, even outside of those lines, were all single mothers raising their children with no fathers. Their primary images of fathers were of those of the children who stood in line at those government facilities.

By now I had spent enough days in those family waiting lines at the county jails to last a lifetime. And my children were now old enough to know where they were going. As if the two-hour drive wasn't enough to deter me, the thought of their childhood memories being that of their father as a man behind a glass partition just shuddered my bones. No matter how many other children were standing there waiting to see their fathers, brothers, uncles, and cousins it was not a place I chose for my children to remember their father.

I know how memories can taunt a soul. And no matter the "pretty picture" those families had on visiting day the energy of those moments were never all that pretty.

Now I know there is always a story. There is always an excuse and this is always his first time. Or even more, this was just the system trying to set an example of what was really not his fault. You see that's why I couldn't look those women in the eyes anymore. I told those stories, too. I believed those stories. That used to be my truth, too. This was his first time, [most of them meant in trouble at all]. It was a really minor offense. No one's helping him. He's sick. He just needs help.

Let me tell you from plenty of personal experience. From living in those lies and emerging from the veil. No one just ends up in jail on accident. Not even when it really is a "minor" offense and his/her first time in. There is plenty of behavior that leads up to getting caught. Which is really all jail means; they got caught for behavior that is currently the norm of their existence. Respect never leads anyone near situations that would land them in jail. Anything less than honoring yourself, and thus all those around you, just isn't respectful. To the self most of all. Every pretty color of paint in my damn pallet couldn't cover up the truth of my canvas to anyone who lives outside the veil.

You see it wasn't just about the feeling and memories my children would have. I just couldn't stand to look into the eyes of all those women standing in line. The ones who drove an hour, to be there two hours before, checking in, leaving commissary, checking the status, and waiting and waiting and waiting. Waiting for a 30-60 minute visit often behind glass, sitting on a rather small [and I am really petite], very cold metal stool, talking through a phone that may or may not work, and has certainly been used by God-only-knows who before you. A million of my little alcohol swabs were not going to get clean those clogged receivers, giving me very clear messages if only I would listen.

Considering the truth of the women in that culture, or denial as such, were no longer my own. That mirror began to fade from my view. The women who'd mirrored back a common truth for so long no longer had a message to reflect back to me. The message I chose to hear and the eyes I began to look into were that of my own. As we begin to look into our own eyes those looking back begin to shift as well.

Looking from behind the veil revealed so much more now. I was no longer interested in the lies. I was no longer interested in looking at the truth through their eyes, his eyes. I could no longer deny it and he was still dead in the middle of it. Not only living cloaked in fear and denial, but actually building layers and layers of bricks around himself ensuring it was good and solid now that everything around it was crumbling.

Although it was Christmas, my bleeding heart of compassion was screaming and my own inner terror of a fatherless family at my favorite holiday was raging, I was damn sure not going to set one more foot in that line of denial again! My children were not going to build memories of a life they had no right to and a lie they didn't need to live through. That was the last time my sons would see their father behind bars even if it was the last time they would see him. It was the last time I would stand in line comforting women with our eyes, and swooning the screaming children waiting for memories that would haunt them for a lifetime they had yet to live.

I had no idea what that meant at the time. Today I know it was another step. It was a practice.

This was my first practice in surrender. Whatever the attempt looked like it was still surrender and that's all that mattered.

Pregnant with our third child and going into my favorite holiday of the year; one that my own *Leave it to Beaver* style family had erected as this monumental occasion signifying the unity of the family; I bore down and went it alone. Or so I thought at the time.

It was 1am and I could barely hold my eyes open. I was half way through screwing together this *Thomas the Train* table. My boys loved trains. And damn it my parents always put up half the toys, spread out another hundred or so around the room and had socks over flowing their edges. So I was bound and determined to get the table, not only put together, but actually usable. Let's just say it was standing and rather stable by the time I was finished. Putting together and erecting fabulous train stations and cities have never been my strong suit. But somehow I got something that slightly appeared like one together before I collapsed in bed.

Lying there in bed I remembered that Santa usually eats the cookies. I hate milk and yet I love the joy in my children that arises from the fact that fantasies can still be real to them. So I headed down the stairs ate the cookies and poured the milk in the sink. Santa had done "her" job for the night. I cried myself to sleep that night and many more to come as I mourned my belief system that was crumbling before me.

And that's all that really crumbled. A belief system that had me confined to a death trap I myself created and upheld to be truth. As I began to surrender to the truth that is, and was then, rather than hold strong to my constructed ones I needed to be true in order for my self-made realities to be upheld, I began to learn about surrender.

Surrender is so much more than acceptance. Another damn practice I knew nothing about. It's like being pregnant. You can only know so much until you are pregnant yourself. There is something about being in the middle of those God awful pains of morning sickness that reading about them just doesn't give justice to. Surrender is like that, too.

And to top that off, to this day, both acceptance and surrender remind me of those bloomin' onions at *Outback*. They just keep on peeling back, so big and deep that you almost get a stomachache getting all the way to the middle. The middle that you never really get to and always wonder if there is one at all. Layers upon layers remind you that you really don't even know what you don't know. And knowing only comes in the experience of living through it.

Surrender is a lot like that to me. It's just something you live your way through. One moment at a time you just practice and practice. You do what you know when you know it. And when you know better you do better. That's what I did that Christmas. As I accepted the truth as it was. I began to surrender into it.

I chose not to go to those jail cells anymore. I chose to let him sit there even on Christmas. Not because I did not love my husband. But because I was not going to support someone who wasn't supporting himself, and certainly wasn't supporting his family. Tough love grew a new meaning in my life. Even that phrase today makes me laugh. Love is just love and sometimes its tough, sure, but it's not like Tough Love isn't compassionate love. It isn't even the love that's tough. It's the reckoning with the truth it brings us that is often the "tough" part. And even that is only made tough by our desire to fight instead of surrender.

Maybe I was just too tired of fighting. Maybe I had no strength left. Maybe I just didn't have anything left to try. Maybe I just got wise. Either way surrender made its way into my life. And although it's taken years to take hold, it began way back then. It started with the practice of honoring me and in that, honoring all those around me, by living into the truth of what just was in my life.

Surrendering, although not really explainable with words, is best metaphored for me through nature. There is a reason why they recommend going downstream instead of paddling up. There is a reason why bridges are built with sway in them to adjust and integrate with the natural course of wind. There is a reason why rain falls and then evaporates to fall again. There is a reason why so many elements of physical structure have to accommodate for the flow of natural tendencies.

Why I ever thought me, and my life, would be the exception is beyond me. As if I could erect structures and belief systems that were rock solid, and think the flow would just go around me while I stood tall, strong and solid in the face of it. Life is not particle or wave, but simultaneously both. Quantum physics proves this over and over again.

As I began to reckon with my truth, surrender came alive for me. Some things you just have to flow with in order to come out alive. You can either keep chipping away at a steel wall or you can reach to the right, turn the door knob and walk right through the door. This time, I chose the door knob.

Shift. . . Shift. . .

In the basket I had on the left side of my bed was the book I was reading at the time. Reading always made me tired again. I thought it may put me back to sleep on that restless night. I picked it up and turned to the section where I left off.

Surrender was the topic. I took a deep breath. Facing the wall, on your knees, with your hands tied behind your back, about to be executed didn't have to come on the streets of New York at the hands of the mob or in the dirt paths found in Latin America. There are many ways to be brought to surrender in your life. I knew it well. Facing the walls on my knees, hands tied behind my back, that is. I am sure you know it well yourself.

Some of us know it when our husbands come home. Others know it when the bill collector comes. Some know it when we speak to ourselves, maybe even in the voices of our screaming kids reflecting ourselves back to us. Yet others know it at the hands of physical illness. And yes, some know it, through the terror inflicted on us by strangers both random, and deliberate.

Truth

There is no actual terror outside of us. That's right there are no bad guys out to get us. No terrorist trying to get into our country. There are no killers, rapists and burglars. There aren't even evil spirits or dark entities out to get us. The "evil" we experience in the world is the horror we harbor within ourselves. All we are is all we see.

If you see terror it's simply a mirror reflecting back to you that which you feel inside. What you feel is an indication of what you hold within, what you "are". If you see it. It's because you validated its existence in your life by "knowing" it.

When all you are is love; when all you know is love. When you know love is all there is; love is all you will experience. When you accept all things, at all times, with no exceptions at all through the act of living such, you will see acceptance reflected around you.

We are that which we see in the world. To affect the world around you, affect the world within you. Live that which you wish to see, experience and feel. Taking this to the "extreme" action you think I am speaking about will create the extreme results you are seeking!

I am now clear that life is a lesson on living, not on life itself. Most of us think the answers to the questions, who am I and why am I here, are life long journeys. Maybe even the point of life itself. Maybe we'll get a glimpse of it upon crossing. Maybe we'll reflect upon it when arriving.

Living who you are and why you are here is the point. Not knowing who we are and why we are here causes more illness than any other disease, crime and war combined and multiplied ten fold! We create crime, disease and war because we do not know who we are and why we are here; that we are pure love and acceptance, and we are here to play, as it is in heaven. The world is our playground.

When we do not know the very unique essence we have and how it makes the world go round. In the face of that, we "loose", or shift, our power.

The Truth of the Raindrop
"I am only one drop anyway! I just get washed away and dried up by the sun." says the raindrop. "Why fall in the first place?"

Think about this, if every raindrop stopped falling because they thought it was pointless there would be no renewal.

If the oceans dry up because the rain stops falling the tides will calm and the wind will stop blowing. The wind will no longer take food to little varmints and varmints will no longer feed animals.

> *"A butterfly flapping its wings in Brazil will affect the wind currents in North America."*
> *Author unknown*

When the raindrop knows it falls amongst others creating renewal it finds meaning in falling. It finds meaning in evaporating. It finds meaning in releasing, washing away, and all the other things that happen because of this raindrop.

Granted raindrops are not human. Only humans seem to need meaning. When kneeling at that wall facing the grayness of it all, with our hands tied behind our backs we seem to need a reason to be there. As if when it has a reason, then I can surrender to it.

I was in my eighth week of a third pregnancy. One that came in the middle of a storm with little excitement and a lot of fear. By the eighth week I had surrendered to the life growing inside of me, and the reason it may be here. I kept repeating my mantra; the will of God will never take me where the grace of God cannot hold me.

At 28, already single, with the third child from my ex-husband on its way I looked at my 2 year old and my 3 ½ year old and thought, Why God Why? How can I handle more?

I sat in the waiting room of my Dr.'s office watching all these women wait their turn. There was the mother in her six month excited about the possibility of a new family member. There was the mother in her 8 ½ month just wanting the life outside of her instead of inside! There was the woman holding her newborn with smiles on her face and joy in her heart. There was the woman with frazzled hair and stress in her eyes as she calmed her 4 year old that was having a tiff with her 6 year old. And there was the woman sitting to my left, about 35, no wedding ring and no children to speak of, a little in awe of it all.

Then there was me, picking up a Parent magazine, looking at the photos of infants, mothers and families in their various stages. I began to feel a tingle of excitement in my heart. Life is joyful no matter the circumstances.

In one hour I was listening to my Dr. tell me the other heart inside of me had stopped beating.

I was presented with another one of those times where we look for meaning. Another moment of surrender had arisen. Surrendering had new meaning again.

Shift. . . Shift. . .

Rather than understand the meaning, I simply accepted there was one. Life has this delicate balance about it. When you connect to your center you really do connect to the center of life its self. Life really does pump inside each of our physical beings. Power truly exists in each of our spirits. All we need exists within us. All we are, we already are.

The raindrops really do fall into the ocean. The tides of the ocean really do affect the wind. The wind really does carry food to animals. Animals really do fertilize the soil that grows the plants we eat.

When I surrender to the process of life and allow myself to be led by it or flow with it, meaning emerges in the integration. It's like that puzzle you tried to piece together on the table with your grandmother when you were six. There was one piece missing on the edge. The beautiful picture that puzzle has to show is skewed without that little piece on the edge.

Even the horrors of our lives, the shameful moments and hurtful events have their place. They have their meaning, their reason.

Surrender leads back to acceptance, as acceptance leads back to surrender. When we don't accept what is right in front of us for what it is we forget to honor the purpose it has. We lose pieces to the puzzle. The beautiful picture it displays is not quite as beautiful without those pieces. It is not our place to make something more or less of those pieces than they are right now. Sometimes we have to step back and remember it's not the pieces that are always so beautiful but the picture it displays when connected to each other.

Power really does emerge in the integrated connections to each other. Surrendering honors the wisdom that each piece was made to connect to another in order to display a very beautiful picture. We may not be privileged to it, right now. We may never be privileged to it. But each raindrop that falls does flow into the ocean. The tides of the ocean do make the wind blow.

And the wind currents in North America will affect that butterfly flapping its wings in Brazil, even though they never see each other. It starts with the butterfly flapping its wings because it has them, and it can. Surrendering sometimes to the fact that it's just enough to live their unique life. Knowing it is all they are here to do and the planet would not be the same if they didn't. Whether or not they always see or know the difference it makes.

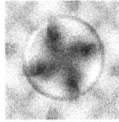

Faith is what you have when you don't quite "know" yet. When surrendering is still a process and yet to be a part of you. It's what I turned to when even opening the door brought a bit of fear. I mean what's on the other side of that door anyhow? At least I knew what chipping away at the steel was like. At least I knew the pain well and had created methods of dealing with the pain it caused.

Shift. . . Shift. . .

The pain had been increasing over the weekend. But I was strong and the kids were with their grandparents. I curled up in the fetal position I had been in for 28 years, wrapped myself in a blanket and zoned out to the TV. I breathed through the pain, meditated as I needed to and called my friend one state over for extra support. She always made everything better, no matter how far away she was.

Screaming at the top of my lungs with pain I thought would certainly kill me this time, was how I woke up the next day though. I couldn't stand. I couldn't sit. I couldn't move at all. I could barely find enough strength to even scream or breathe. The tears were just frozen in my tear ducks. They couldn't even roll down my face.

And let me tell you I'd had severe endometriosis for 15+ years by this point. I lived in horrid pain three weeks out of every month for as long as I could remember. The kind of pain that left me sitting with heating pads in both the front and back on my mid-section and monthly doses of vicadin I only took on the worst day of the month in order to prevent the habit forming medication from taking hold. I delivered two children by c-section and they weren't the only surgeries I'd had interspersed between emergency room visits several times a year for abdominal pain as a child. So I knew stomach pain well.

Now, I thought for sure I was dying. This was it. It had all caught up to me now.

I managed to dial my mother-in-law who convinced me to dial 911. The ambulance and a huge fire truck with six paramedics got there just before she did.

Two days earlier I had my first check up for our third child only to find out her heart had stopped beating in her eighth week of life. Coming out of the check up room a nurse met me to notify me that because the baby was already dead I also couldn't qualify for temporary state medical aide for pregnant mothers with no health insurance. A combination of a pre-existing condition and self-employment, with all its freedoms, left me without health insurance.

Once again I chose to go it alone. I'd pass the baby at home then. That was of course until I woke up feeling like I was dying. Which I guess has some merit considering that's what I was passing, death. And I was passing it in so many more ways than one. They rushed me to the ER where they did an emergency "D and C". Removing all the remnants I had yet to pass. I had passed much of the baby on my own. There was just that last little bit having trouble leaving my body.

Boy did I know about that! Death had a hard hold on me in so many ways. My body just simply didn't know how to let it all go. To surrender into the truth. To let pass what had already passed.

Yes at times like this we turn to faith. My husband was a drug-addicted, alcoholic diagnosed bi-polar, psychisophrenic man in jail. When he wasn't, he was stalking me. Christmas had just passed and so had my third child. I was now a single mother, more than one statistic and I had earned it all in less than one year. [Deep Breath]

In this process of surrender, faith was my friend. What do you do when you lose everything you thought you had only to learn it wasn't even real in the first place? What do you do when you learn the "reality" you thought you had was only a construct you created?

Testaments were all I listened to. Clichés were all I spoke. "The sun rises after it sets." "If it doesn't break you it makes you stronger." I practiced them day in and day out. They became my mantra, like the prayers, Let go and Let God, and the Serenity Prayer.

Faith, like life, has its ups and downs. It remains only because we've yet to reconcile the truth in our souls. Once truth takes hold, it's all there is. Faith becomes a memory of the bridge that got us to the truth we are now.

Surrender is the walk across that bridge of faith. You just put one foot in front of the other. You step from the ground you are on to the one you see ahead.

Even though you see it ahead of you, it's not really beneath your feet. It's not really the same grounding that stables the one still planted. And yet you use faith to remind you that the grounding you have now, came from taking the step before it. To remind you that the ground beneath you now, once appeared like the one that stands in front of you.

Not all bridges are "sturdy" like you understand sturdy, either before you enter the bridge or even on the bridge. They all have their "weak" points, or at least what appears like weak points when you are standing on the bridge. Sometimes it may even feel like you fall. You may. It may feel like you stumble. You may. It may feel like you are lost. You may be. The walk may feel like you are doing it alone, with no compass, guidance or map. You may be.

Faith is what gets you across. Believing is what puts the bounce in your step. It's the fuel to your vehicle. However, with every step, with every practice of surrender, you begin to replace faith with truth, belief with being.

I may Be today. I may live in my truth today. And my onion is still bloomin'. The bridge only arrived at a dock that led me to a ship that has set sail in the ocean of my existence in a world where surrender is a constant wave that sometimes crashes against the fiberglass of my yacht. At other times, rides me to the shores of the ports I visit.

When sailing for the first time the waves seem to crash more often and feel harsher than they may be. You have this vision of them flipping this beautiful ship you just received right over backwards. Back to where you got "her" from. Landing you right back on that bridge from which you came. Flowing in the waves of the ocean doesn't often feel all that flowing at first.

It takes a minute for our bodies to adjust to the motion of the ocean. To flow with the natural tenants of the universal flow. We have to practice surrender. Going back to that onion. The layers just keep peeling. Just when you think you've rode out a wave, another comes rolling in. Our bodies are used to being still and solid. Once thrown into the movement of the tides, even with their clock-work flow, it takes us a minute to adjust to their timing instead of our own.

It was the middle of the day, late summer in Southern California. It was warm outside, the sun was shining, but the day seemed dreary for me as usual. The kids were in school and I was home, at "work".

Lying on my bed, in my room, I looked to the right, out the window. It over looks my back yard, most of which is a hill rich with nature. With a clean lens it pours tranquility into a busy life smack in the middle of a city. It speaks harmony to those who listen. It allows you to cohabitate with Mother Earth's offspring; plants, trees, flowers, hummingbirds, two bluebirds, a family of rabbits and an occasional coyote. You can even smell the ocean breeze on a windy day!

That day was lacking tranquility, though. Peace was absent. Fear was ever present! I saw eyes looking back at me and they weren't from Mother Earth. I didn't want to open my own eyes. I didn't want to get up. I didn't want to breathe.

I glanced at the clock as the day seemed to fade away minute, by minute. I thought on one hand it couldn't go by fast enough. On the other hand, the faster the day went the sooner I'd have to get the kids from school. At that point I'd have to emerge from the sheets for a few hours. I'd have to make do at living until they went to bed again.

I found myself at a point in life where I couldn't find a reason to wake up. I couldn't find a reason to live. Not even my boys, the two little angels in my life, were reason enough for me to go through the day. At that point, choice became palpable power.

I got up that morning only to find myself lying in that fetal position again. Laying right in front of my closet door screaming at the top of my lungs, rocking back and forth, asking why, why, why???

As I began to bring my breathing back to a rhythm and loosen the grip on my eyes shut so tightly, I realized I was at least outside of my closet door. Now to some that may not have any significance at all. To a child who hid in her closet crying for hours on end when "trauma" hit her, this was significant. To all the closet criers, you know what I mean.

I thought, at least I am not in the God damn closet! I may be curled up in the fetal position. I may be wailing like a child and praying for death to find me as it had found my last child, but damn it I was not in the closet!!

Some significance just has to come as simple as that. I thought, I am not in the closet. Then I began to realize, well actually, I am pretty alive, too.

Yes, that's right, every fear I had got manifested into my "reality", and I am still alive. Not only am I alive, but I still own a rather successful business that I operate while setting my own time, location and schedule. I am no longer married and a single mother. Even though I might lose it next month, this month I have a roof over my head. And a rather beautiful four-bedroom home that smelled like salt water while standing in the back yard on a breezy afternoon in a Southern California paradise. My kids were right now in a very wonderful private Montessori school. My husband was locked up and far from hurting me today. Although they were several states away, I had some of the best friends most people only dream of having and are blessed if they have one. I had several.

So considering I was still alive, all my fears had come true and I was still so incredibly blessed - what did that mean? For me it cemented that fear really is an illusion. Love was the only thing that existed for me.

Something, that had until then, only been read in books now became my new reality. I had a choice lying there. I could either hold tight to those fears that didn't seem to have such a tough face anymore, or I could just stand up and get over it.

Yes I know, after all that drama, it had really become that simple for me, and that instant. Although, it was not that easy. It was as simple as surrendering my reality as I knew it then and living into truth. The truth that love really is all there is.

When you come to a knowing of a love like that in your life, of a presence that is so much greater than yourself, you really do fall to your knees. Considering I was well past being on my knees, and in fact curled up clutching mine, I just stayed there!

After years of abuse, which really just meant I had forgotten my power, my choice required that I remember it or surrender life all together.

Many of us are brought to similar points in our life. They don't have to be as traumatic as mine were that day. They don't have to bring us to the brink of life or death, but they can if we don't take the opportunities along the way to reclaim ourselves and live our power when the choices present themselves.

To surrender I had to stop giving life to my fears. They had all come true anyhow, and I was still standing there.

I began to wake up each morning with hope for a new beginning. I began to sit at my desk each morning. I began to smile at people in passing cars as I took the kids to school. I began to shower and get dressed for my day, whether or not I got out of the house. I not only joined the PTO, but got elected president. I took clients that required me to be in their office again. I took yoga classes. I began to date. I essentially put myself out in the world again. In order to breathe life I began to live. With no idea how I just said yes. I made a conscious choice, and took conscious action.

In addition to putting myself out there again, I had to shift the way I thought. I had to shift the way I treated myself. Surrendering meant conscious action, even when no one was looking. This was the most difficult.

In the dark of the night, when the kids went to bed and the moon shone over that hill by my bed side I had to know I was safe without someone telling me. I had to overcome the demons in my own mind that abused me more than the next person.

I began to honor myself. I began to love me, by caring about me, my time, needs and interests. I took responsibility for myself and retrained my mind. I set, and stood by, very clear boundaries. I began respecting myself by clarifying what my priorities of the moment were. I let go of the responsibility of others.

Today, I still run a successful business. I support myself, and two boys, in an upper middle class environment. My boys still attend a private Montessori school. We enjoy a few pleasures here and there. We live modestly, yet comfortably. In addition, I still have debt to pay off, challenges to overcome, and fears that creep up. My waves keep crashing and they keep taking me to new and beautiful ports as well.

The difference today, versus five years ago when the same was true, is my perspective of it. Surrendering did not give me the material life I had, and still have. It gave me back myself. It gave me an attitude of gratefulness. It gave me joy, peace and a perspective of abundance. I live harmoniously and powerfully today.

You see, I "remembered" my power by releasing all that covered me, removing my veils of denial and surrendering to truth whether or not I always understood it. I connected with the center of who I am. I know, with utter clarity, what my unique essence is.

Shift. . . Shift. . .

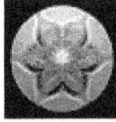

Surrender is a practice until it becomes a way of being. And it does become a way of being. Surrender doesn't mean that one day the waves stop crashing, that the flow even gets smooth all the time. Remember those waves that just keep coming? And the faith that got you across the bridge? In the boat, faith is replaced by trust.

Trust is much different than faith. Faith is a believing until you see it. Trust is a knowing, because although you can't see it now and may never see it at all, you know it is. And in that knowing it dissipates altogether. Trust is your anchor in the middle of storms that hit the seas of the oceans you sail in.

To this day I'm not exactly sure if it's what leads you out, brings the sunshine out to dry up the rain or is telling us it wasn't really a storm in the first place.

Shift. . . Shift. . .

At first trust came in the form of remembering. What doesn't kill you really does make you stronger. I use those memories, like the one of me curled in front of the closet, to hold me in times ahead when the waves keep on crashing. I remembered the epiphany I had, that even when all my fears came true I was still held in love, still safer than ever and now even more abundant and solid. I still hold strong to that memory when I need to trust in the middle of a "raging storm".

Those memories help me learn how to trust. Because I did know. I have more than faith to lean on now. I just have to remember in those dark moments, what the light was like and how it found me every time.

Practicing trust like this shows me how practicing merges you with truth. It really is a merging. There is a truth about us that always is. Whether or not we recognize it, accept it or surrender into it is a whole 'nother thing. Who I am today is not new. It's not revolutionary. It's quite simple.

The me that's here on this plane, often referred to as personality and character, just found the rest of me on various other planes, like my spirit, my soul, and the grander energy we refer to as oneness. All of those parts simply found each other, reconciled and remembered each other. As I chose to surrender into that it became to the naked eye what it always has been.

We call this process transmutation. Which is when the individual parts of a whole come together, and in that coming together, or mixture, they transmute each individual part, as well as the whole simultaneously. Thus transmutation. In simple terms its really just reconciliation, but it feels and looks an awful lot like transmutation. Which it is often hard to reconcile. [Smiles] Again it has a lot to do with where you are standing and the view you have from the "place" with which you are.

When reconciliation or transmutation occurs truth "becomes" you. It's all you know and all you are. Not only do faith and belief become unnecessary but so does trust. They become bridges that you crossed, to a knowing, that is past the stage of remembering for you.

It's like standing in that garden of your meditation where the greens are incredibly lush, the flowers bright and blooming. Where the colors are full and the smell so fresh. Where there is plenty of laughter and joy. Where children are playing and the air is so light you can fly. When just being there makes you feel held and all that exists is love. Where there are no words for love because the opposite never existed. Where love is the only truth there is.

Shift. . . Shift. . .

Sitting on the ledge of this cement wall that holds up the alley climbing the hill to the pier I sat watching the waves roll in and out. I was barely 21. And although I had seen the ocean once before, it was from the deck of a boat as large as Vegas Hotels. There is something magnificent about the forms of nature that dwarf us in comparison. They have a power to humble even the boldest parts of our egos.

For me, they also had the power to wash away all the fear, anger and pain that would rush through me like the waves that mesmerized me at the time. I sat on that ledge daily, sometimes at 2am. When I couldn't find peace in my sleep I found it in those waves. There were two buildings between our two bedroom apartment and the grand Pacific Ocean. I had dreamed of living at the ocean since I was little. There was such a grand difference, at the time, between that view from the ledge I dangled my legs over, between the parking lot and the ocean, and the fence I dangled my legs over on the fields of the Mid-West.

Those fields that lead from one, to another, to another were surely as vast. But for me personally, there was just something about the rolling tides that seemed to take all the worries out to sea. Out to a place I was sure only God lived. To a place where Mother Earth gobbled them up and transformed them back into the love from which they came.

My grandmother has, for years upon years, sat in this big old burly orangish, brown chair in her kitchen.

Looking out a huge picture window. It over looks her barnyard that leads to field, after field, after field only obstructed by an interstate that streams cars to and fro. It too, overlooked the West. Where the sun set on day, after day.

To her, those rolling fields and the swaying of the corn tassels in the Mid-Western wind took away her worries too. God had some place, far into the horizon, that set over the corn and soybean fields in the plains of Illinois. A place where Mother Earth could also recycle the fears, anger, pain and worry that are just part of our human existence.

Today it's peaceful to know that no matter where you are, or what vision you see, there is a place for us all. A place where the horizon seems to swallow the concerns of our soul into the gut of a God we all name, define and understand differently, but performs the same task for us all.

Now I can sit at the edge of those corn fields with a different understanding of their very own vastness. One that lacks any kind of comparison to the ocean that rode far out to the horizon over that tall cement wall. Because there is no comparison to what likens to such similarity.

The mountains that surround the vast desert valley I reside in today have their own powerful message, too. I've come to know that no matter where you are the East can raise a power within you. The West can swallow that which you wish to purge. Anything vast, made of the very earth energy that we are too, can replenish anything back to the love from which it arose.

Kaleidoscope   139

That truth I found in my life, the trust I practiced to get there, arose out of that reckoning in me. The reckoning that my grandmother, sitting in her big burly, orange chair that simply smelled like stale coffee and smokey cigarettes, overlooking a field that was nothing short of boring to me has brought her the very same peace that I got from the ocean. From, what to her, was a big hard, cement wall overlooking an overcrowded parking lot that obscured a natural setting filled with the noise of a city that spoke silence and serenity to me.

The point isn't the setting. The point is the peace we find within ourselves through a vastness provided by Mother Nature in all her glory. From the Pacific Ocean to the mountains of the Rockies, from the fields of Illinois to the mouth of the Mississippi in the Gulf, from the Southern porches to the North Atlantic coast line; there is peace in it all if we choose to see it.

The setting isn't the point. The purging done through forgiveness is what brings us peace. The vast glory of Mother Nature herself is the simple reminder to find forgiveness in our hearts. Nothing is as big as the grander picture of life. The 'will' we have and the life we see is nothing compared to that of the Energy that is the earth we live upon. From my grandmother's picture window, to the ledges of the ocean and the valley at the base of a circle of mountains, the message is still the same. Nothing is as big as they. And everything can be swallowed into the gut of the earth and regurgitated back as the life force it really is.

It simply takes a moment to let it go. To find forgiveness, in order to release the hold any lie has on you. In releasing the lies to the waves of forgiveness, they promise to take them back to the sea from which they came.

Small town America was peace and silence to my family. Everyone knew everyone. The land held onto energy from generation, upon generation of the same DNA strands. The small amount of people who knew your entire line of DNA from your great-grandparents to your children's children was not peace to me, though. There was very little privacy, and thus silence, for me.

This disparaging difference in our visions and understanding of what lay in front of us, our inability to see the view from each other's vantage point, has not only been a thorn in the side of a grip of core relationships meant to root a child, but has also prevented us from accepting each other for years.

There in lies the root of my anger and my start in a journey to love. The journey paved with a requirement of ongoing forgiveness, delivering me to trust, resulting in the love I am today. A journey that has been long and full of storms, just like yours and the others sitting around you. A journey that only felt that way because I chose to hear and see it that way. A journey that still remains the same, only the ship I sail in has shifted. The captain aboard is guiding the ship with the guidance of the will that guides us all. And the sight is so much different.

How did I arrive at the place of Love? How did I get to that meditation garden that manifested in the earth of my existence here on this plane? How did trust find its way into my life? The trust that led to me to the experience of love.

That journey started long before the long jail lines to see an abusive husband with a horrid drug problem. The start may have landed me in those lines. It may have led me to my own misguided entrepreneurship that grew long before Corporate America. It may have resulted in a life of single motherhood and bankruptcy before 30. But at the core it's really about a process of acceptance, found through an experience of judgment.   The kind that requires forgiveness in order to release the anger those oceans used to wash away.

Through time you begin to know, that the fields my grandmother saw through her picture window and the oceans I saw from my cement wall are only momentary cleansers of an anger born out of the forgotten truth that always was, still is, all I need to be.

From the point of forgetting, to the point of knowing, to the dock of being love, you have this 'journey' that becomes a ride even once you get 'there'. . .

It has a different face for us all. We call it by different names. We experience it through different stories. But the through line, even the climax, tends to be the same. Just like I learned the common through line of those corn fields and the ocean I longed for since I was a child. Today the beauty and power in them both are still the same. As are the faces, names and stories we put on our pain until we learn it's always been love.

Still the process is necessary. Being only happens by

living through the story that is our own. The beauty in this wisdom is found in the common through lines. Common patterns beneath what appears to us like the chaos of our oceans. The waves that seem to keep crashing. When we can find these through lines, we know we are closer to merging with the truth of the pattern that is common in us all.

But how do we get there? How do we emerge from "chaos" and fall into the flow of the patterns?

Listen.

Silence yourself and just listen. . . Can you hear that?

"Can you hear that?" I asked my son. "Listen carefully." I told him.

He said, "Mommy, I don't hear anything."

We were driving in a 17-foot U-Haul; my two young sons, both under five, with car in tow on our second consecutive trip to Vegas, in a moving truck packed to the limits, with items even stacked on the top of the car we were pulling. Some of us tend to accumulate more than others!

I said, "It's calling us! Can you hear it?"

He exclaimed for the second time, "Mommy I can't hear anything!" He was completely bewildered why we were moving from such a beautiful and serene home in Southern California to a place in the middle of a hot desert.

He said, "Mommy I don't want rocks in my back yard!"

My grander point was that life speaks to us all the time. It gives us direction when we listen. When we choose to silence ourselves. When we merge into the flow it will speak very clearly to us. Anger, fear, resentment, rage, sadness, pain, the whole lot of them are all very loud voices speaking very clear messages to us if we choose to listen. Each of them leading us closer to the life of love that is the only truth there is.

We often choose not to listen. We choose to fight instead of surrender. Many times in my life I chose to fight instead of flow.

"Flow like the ocean, flow, flow flow!" Were the words of a very special activity my children and I do. We would wave our hands in the air simulating the waves of the ocean, moving our entire bodies like lose spaghetti. We'd laugh and giggle until more than our bodies were lose and limber.

It was created to help my older son go with the flow of life. He chose to hang on to the past quite tightly as we moved from a life of "chaos" to a life of truth. As a small child everything he knew was pulled out from beneath him in a matter of months. Even though it was unhealthy, it was still all he knew and happened to take away from him a very prized love found in his father.

The ocean activity was created for him, but let me tell you it guided me to the flow as much as him. Visual and physical reminders are always great guidance to the truth. From the flowing ocean activity I did with my children, to the ocean that cleansed me, and the fields that calmed my grandmother releasing is the practice. Forgiveness is its name.

You only get to trust by releasing the anger, pain, hurt, sadness, rage and fear we hold inside as the "truth". It feels like the truth. Really they are only constructs we build to keep hold of the "safety" we feel we need. A safety that is built on lies and not at all safe.

Another practice, right! Another practice, that at the time, I too, had no idea what it looked like. Release the anger. What do I throw it in, the ocean? Do I forget I have it? Do I say it's not real when the firm flesh of it suffocates me?

Let me tell you trust is arrived at by sailing the waters of forgiveness, which leads you to freedom. The kind of freedom where all that is right now is all it ever has been and all there really is. Truth, at this point of liberation, has a strength that removes all that is not.

Getting there may be simple. It's far from easy. Especially when you know nothing of it.

Shift. . . Shift. . .

Hindsight is often clearer than foresight. Forgiveness is often easier to find when the blessing arrives. Let me tell you, though, the blessing arrives swifter if you search for the forgiveness first. The truth is, the blessing has always been, you just have to find it. The surest way is through forgiveness.

Forgiveness may be simple. Let go, right!? A lack of forgiveness is simply holding onto a lie that isn't real anyway. Control is another word for it. Doesn't mean it's always easier! I can certainly witness that too.

As I walked in the door through the garage there they lay. Naked and sprawled out all over MY living room. Crack head, after crack head. The two of them entangled in each other. Beer bottles spread out all over the house!

As I leapt for him, she leapt for the bathroom to the right, hiding from a rage I didn't even know I had myself. Phones flying, words soaring, him now chasing me. Three cracked out drug addicts, having a sex-infested affair in the broken into home of the woman they are scorning, now full of more rage than she ever knew she had, leaves for a messy setting. A 911 call later, crashed cars in a driveway and three, now lunatics, yelling and chasing each other were the state of that moment.

3am, later that night, racing down the freeway, dodging in and out of cars - If I had not lost my mind by now I certainly had that night! Fear can certainly do funky things to a person. Now, I have racing blood in my family, but this was no racetrack. The man in front of me was not driving a formula one, or a late model. Neither of us were in safety gear.

When anger and resentment this deep rise to the surface safety gear is the last thing on your mind. There was a lot to forgive. Stolen money, time and again. From broken glass, to breaking and entering. Affairs, drugs, abuse, you name it, it happened. Left with two kids, a mountain of debt and a broken spirit that leaked into a worn out physical health was what my marriage blessed me with at that moment. Everything a man can do to a woman. Everything one human can do to another, to defy the other, was heaped on my plate of forgiveness requirements. All that simply piled on the anger and resentment that overflowed the cup that sailed me there in the first place.

With all that man had chosen to do, having an affair was certainly the breaking of the feeble back that held us up. Finding the reflection of it in my home was more than a climax. If there was one more line to cross when it came to integrity in our marriage, it had now been crossed.

Anger had reached the point of rage. Whatever ounce of sanity was left in my blood had far boiled out that day.

If I hadn't learned forgiveness yet I was either gonna learn it now, or suffocate from the mounting resentment. I have a tendency to learn things in a BIG way. I always ask for the lessons clearly and swiftly. Careful what you wish for!

Hindsight is even clearer than a crystal clear vision of the moment. They say Rome wasn't built over night, but it can be torn down in a moment. This past year a Tsunami in Southeast Asia and a category five hurricane in our own American Gulf coast proved that. Not that Mother Nature and all her glory haven't shown that over and over again in tornados and earthquakes in other parts of the world for centuries. Every once in a while we all need a little reminding.

What was the lesson? Where was the blessing? I prayed to find it so I could move onto forgiveness. The resentment was stealing every last breath I had. All the deep breaths and hours of yoga in the world were not gonna relieve this pain. Sitting at the edge of the ocean was certainly not gonna get it done either. Hell, I couldn't even sit still I had so much rage boiling inside of me.

Where was I gonna find forgiveness in the middle of this? How could there be a silver lining in this raging storm? I thought there had to be more clouds than silver lining to cover them!

Shift. . . Shift. . .

It was dark, in the middle of the night again. The only light was that of the moon, shining in from the large picture window to the right. The moon rose over the hill behind my house. From my bedroom window all you could see was that hilltop, full of nature's growth, lit up by the full moon ahead.

I just stared out that window. My eyes blurred over from the tears, burning from the length of time they had been streaming down my face by now. I fought past the swollen skin to see the light shining in my room. I often clung to that light, the smell of the salt water blowing in from the breeze and the sounds of that growth on Mother Nature's hill.

Mother Nature has always spoken to me in her many ways. One woman to another, of the faith there is in life. She always taught me that the smallest things are grand when they connect. When you look at the integration of life you understand the instances. Even the simple fact that the plants growing on that hill always grow toward the sun without any guidance at all is testament to the power comprised within the miracle of life.

The waves have been a savior for me, too. You see, the ocean reminds me that the tears falling down my face are tiny. And yet they fall from me like the rain does the sky. Each raindrop may be tiny, but they end up in that large ocean, making waves of their own.

Sitting on that bed, that night like many, like the ones spent dangling my feet over the ledge above the ocean. Or the ones spent in salty silence when I was eight, on the waves beneath me. That night was like so many. Sitting there wondering why I was there. Why had life brought me here? How could I find a way out? How did I end up here in the first place? So connected to life and yet so far from it's breath.

There are women [And men and children, etc.] sitting in their beds across America wondering how they got there, why and where they could go from there. Feeling trapped in the walls that bind them, with no locks on the doors. They are wondering "Why did I end up in a place, called home, that I fear so much? Wasn't home supposed to bring safety? Isn't shelter supposed to shelter us?"

From the little girls of the Taliban to those starving in Cairo. From the women of India to the mothers of China. From the teenagers lying in beds not their own to the 40-year-old women lying in beds alone. There are women all over this world who could prosper from connecting to the breath they have inside of them.

Sure there is terror in our world. There is terror on our streets and even worse there is terror in our homes. The worst terror of all is that found in our hearts, and the corners of our spirit. With all the tears streaming down the faces of our people, no wonder the world is two-thirds water!

Still, that night, I lay in my bed, with my covers to my neck as if they'd keep me from my own terror. I prayed for the light of that moon to shine within me, instead of just on me. I wanted to feel the warmth of that light in my heart. I wanted that light to dry up my tears. I wanted to find my own breath, the one that led me to the sun, like those plants growing on the hill. I wanted to feel my roots and know they were grounded in the soil.

You see plants grow toward the sun naturally. They need no direction or leadership. They need no credentials, titles or money. There is no one telling them how they should and should not grow. They just grow. They simply soak up the nourishment and rev el in the space to grow toward the light.

All these years of staring out into Mother Nature and that's all she was telling me, one woman to another. The power you need is already inside of you. Life grows naturally, all life. It already knows all it needs to know in order to grow. When given the space, and nourished, love/life grows.

When I connect to the center of life within me and then connect to the life around me, life expounds.

Life expounds, or was it me expounding? A little of
both I am sure now. At the point of merger the lines
begin to seem a little hazy. Sanity and insanity that is.
Was it he or I that was seeing things, then or now?

Racing down the highway chasing an illusion. Who
was smoking what? One can now begin to see how
reality and paranoia begin to look an awful lot a like.
Hindsight even began to look a little blurry in the rear
view mirror. Oh God, not another mirror!!!

Nauseous, I was so nauseous again. The tears were
streaming. My head was throbbing. And I was still
racing down the highway literally. Breathe, sister
breathe! As life began to enter my lungs again I made
the familiar middle of the night call that was beginning
to become all too familiar. She knew the drill.

Memories began to flash. . . .

I showed up on the door step at 11pm. We have to
leave now.

"Now?" She asked, looking a bit tired!

"Yes, if we leave right now we'll get there by 3am.
He's high enough to pass out in a couple of hours.
That gives us until early tomorrow morning before he
notices. We can make it there by 3 or 4am and back
here by 10am. With just enough time to run by the
ocean! It's our best chance."

It took her all of five minutes to change her clothes and kiss her own husband goodbye until tomorrow.

He had left on one of his binges again. Not returning back home, one state over, after work on the weekend as promised. On another coke binge, he had called from a friend's. On a binge of my own, bent to end this, I had gone to my trusted best friend, and soul sister.

Someone had to come with me to drive the truck back. I was not paying for his sorry ass, his drug binges and his lies anymore. High on a combination of adrenaline, and hormones from the pregnancy, we drove all the way to San Diego and back to Vegas in less than 12 hours! Snatching the truck in the dark of the night, or morning depending on the perspective, we took one drive by our beloved sister ocean and off we were, back to the city of lights.

Breathe, sister, Breathe. . .

Didn't I shift that damn scope? Why was this picture awfully similar? They say insanity is doing the same things over and over again and expecting a different result. How the hell did I end up here again? And again? And again? Why all of a sudden was this picture so similar?

Forgiveness. . . .

Funny how we can say those words and yet without
the true release of what brought it in, the bags keep
piling up. Somehow we end up going down the same
roads, that may be named a bit differently, but roads
none the less leading to the same dead end. Going
round and round, just racing harder and faster, as the
stakes keep rising, the game gets deeper.

Shift. . . Shift. . .

She "drove" home with me making sure I made it back
to the dungeon of what had now become a hell all
over again. Someone had to drive me home because
I was surely absent.

Shift. . . Shift. . .

Ah yes, I had a lot of letting go to do! A lot of
releasing to get to. A lot to forgive. The house was
packed and it felt terribly empty. The walls I patched
upstairs now had broken windows downstairs where
they had arrived. And the stench of that crystal
remained the same.

Just when I thought the light was seeping back in that
stench came rushing back. There is nothing like a
smell to bring a flood of memories back. I just sat in
the middle of the floor. The wind rushing through the
broken window, new shards of glass covering the

floor. Didn't I just pick this glass up? Didn't I just clean out the house? Is it Groundhog Day again?

Funny thing about surrender, it doesn't actually release what you're holding. It just gets you in the flow. All that stuff you're still holding. . . .If you bring it into the flow with you it's bound to muddy the waters all over again. Yes, you have to do the work of that too. And it too, is just like those Bloomin' Onions. See why I keep getting so nauseous!?

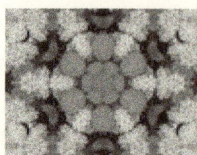

How do you trust after all of that? Couldn't I just go back to the bow of my boat, at the point of dusk, on my beloved ocean, being kissed by the warm summer breezes?

But the cold wind just kept blowing through that broken window. And the next morning I got up and fixed the window. I cleaned up the glass again and fumigated the house. I sold the couch, and bleached the floors, the walls anything else I could find that couldn't be pitched.

Release and purge, release and purge, purge and release. Whatever it took I was gonna let this go. Or the muddy edge to which I was standing was gonna come sliding out from underneath me like the California hills I lived near. And I would go crashing with it.

This time when I repaired those windows I threw out the locks I had placed on them. As they didn't do much good keeping the windows shut when the glass just broke.

I fondly found myself back upstairs in front of that dreaded mirror.

Now I could be angry with her. I could be angry with him. I could be angry with me. I could be angry at a lot of things, and more over a lot of people, those in that moment and the previous ones that came before.

In moments like this we all tend to have a domino recall of all those that piled on before and their velocity somehow tends to add to the thunder of what is falling right now.

The fires all began to flame again, fueled by the wind that had picked up again. I just wanted the fire to be quenched and somehow I couldn't put out the smoldering beneath the flames that kept appearing to go out. With a smoldering beneath, every wind that picked up brought a flame that accompanied it. And the burning just kept getting deeper.

Sometimes they just need to cut it out of you!

Lying on the, oh so familiar floor, curled in my ever comforting fetal position I found the phone to call my friend. The fire that had been burning now made its way to the heart within me that was meant to pump only blood to my body. Clenching my heart like a 60 year old having a heart attack they rushed me to the emergency room.

For thirty days I couldn't stand for more than 2 hours without passing out. I couldn't catch my breath even lying down, my abdomen was the bain of my existence again and my heart still felt like a burning fire a few times a day.

Standing in front of that mirror, now barely able to stand, out of the emergency room with no diagnosis and the life I thought I had found now seeping out of me again, Uhg!

I saw that same vision all over again. I was standing in front of technically a new mirror, but still ceiling to counter top with one on the right and only the wall to the left. The burning I only saw before, I was now experiencing in the core of my body, the heart of my life.

The waves were crashing, the winds were blowing, my eyes were puffy and if only I had the strength I'd be vomiting again.

Releasing can be a long, hard process depending on the road we've traveled, the stuff we've picked up along the way and how hard our grasp to it is. I guess my grasp was tighter and my will stronger than I had imagined. That and it was ground so deep in my soul it would take an excavator to dig it out.

Again, the house we live in can be rebuilt and rebuilt. If we put it back on the same foundation that cracked the walls in the first place. We'll end up right back to the foundation when the wolf huffs and puffs and blows the house down.

Back on the farm, those three little pigs taught me to do the work. Build the house well. A clear foundation often requires us to forgive, or release. I had been practicing this one, forgiveness that was, for plenty longer than the accepting and surrendering. And this one felt worse than the 30 minutes I laid on the floor before the paramedics came to that house when I was letting go of death inside me the last time. And 30 days of pain was much longer than the 20 minutes anyway. Not to mention it was marked by almost 30 years of a disease that marked many of my days.

Forgiveness huh? What does this lead to again? Is all this regurgitating worth it? After I vomit all this up, after all this purging, releasing and forgiving what's gonna be left?

When you hold onto things they grow inside of you. When you leave them unattended, or push them deeper within they begin to take on a life of their own. They attach themselves to your organs, leave adhesions and scaring. They cause all kinds of complications.

Only removing them leaves you healed. Only letting them go leaves you clear. And knowing YOU lie beneath them helps, but when you can't see the ground you're stepping on as you take one step after another going back to faith is sometimes helpful. And step after step, releasing now, as you accept and surrender into it, leads you to a trust that helps truth remain more constant.

Shift. . . Shift. . .

I was standing at the mail box, thumbing through the bills. Searching again for what I had to let go of. Where was that check? The 15th, 17th, 27th, month to month to month I still picked up the phone. I still made that call month after month.

Didn't I already say insanity is doing the same thing over and over again expecting different results? And I wonder why a bi-polar psychitsophrenic stands before me! Reflections, reflections, reflections. . .

Forgiveness is as much a choice as any.

I stood in front of the judge after 18 months of court hearings. Hearing after hearing he never showed up to. I knew if I just gave him enough rope he'd hang himself. 17 months and 2 weeks later he shows himself before her. Ranting and raving about wanting half the assets. Half of the assets that were less than a quarter of the debt and not even close to the required amount to raise two children for 17 more years to come.

"And the children?" she asked.

"Aw, she can have them. I just want my half of our stuff!!" he continued ranting.

She explained he had to go through the proper channels. Fill out the court paperwork and be back in her court room in two weeks she explained.

Tears streaming down my face as I kept reminding myself the rope that chokes, also hangs. Sure enough two weeks later consistency persisted. Standing in that court room alone all over again the judged said, "Ma'am, what would you like?"

I said, "It's in the paperwork. Just give it all to me so I can walk away."

She said, "You can give him half this debt if you wish. He is responsible for it too."

I explained, "It's easier to simply let it go and focus on the clients that are more likely to provide it, than remain in court for years to come trying to get what the "bankrupt" may never have and the irresponsible will never provide."

She clearly understood. As I asked, all the assets, all the debt, full physical and legal custody. She then added sternly, only supervised visitation upon your discretion. She offered me luck and bid me goodbye.

Sometimes we forget the choices we make. Moment to moment we have to keep on making them.

As I stood at that mailbox it hit me again. Forgiveness is not something you do once and it all goes away.

That damn Bloomin' Onion; again, and again, and again.

As I waited for the check that never arrived without several phone calls, at least one fight and getting more involved than it was ever worth, I just made a new choice.

Sometimes one layer of forgiveness just leads to another. One moment, opens up into another. One choice leads to yet another. Forgiveness is a choice until we've peeled away every layer that covers us. Because at the core, where truth lives within us, acceptance is all there is. Where judgment is lacking, love lives and the need for forgiveness of what never really was in the first place doesn't exist.

Until we get there though, the onion keeps on bloomin'. And the need for forgiveness rises to remind us there is more to peel away.

Yes, one day I just choose to walk away again. I chose to let it go, regardless. Regardless! Whether or not the check comes. Whether or not he phones on their birthday. Whether or not he even returns the calls they make. Whether or not he calls in a day of glory to come riding in, if only for a two minute call. Whether or not I have the money to pay the bills. Whether or not there is a clear path today.

Moving on. . .

Forgiveness is often more than letting go. It's an action. An action of stepping out of where you stand and moving on. Moving on to where, you don't often know. All you have to do is say yes. Yes to love. Yes

to a clear space. Yes to flow. Yes. Just yes.
Because anything that holds, blocks the flow.
Releasing that hold, forgiveness through practice,
begins to be more than a clearing. It soon becomes a
moving, a flowing.

A little different than the falling found in surrendering,
that feels like flowing at the time. Forgiveness leads
to a smoothness so flowing; it doesn't always feel like
moving. But it is.

Sooner or later you just find yourself standing in a
different place. And that hindsight brings sight to the
blessings that you thought you might have missed
before! That place becomes a clear space.

Challenges are just challenges. It's how we perceive them that begins to set a course for the power they take on in our lives. The point of the seemingly challenging sides of my cycles, shared here, are not in whether or not they were good or bad, right or wrong that is. Those are only judgments; good or bad, right or wrong. Only when we release the judgments, attachments, do we allow for the space where Truth appears. Only here does power breathe life.

The point, is the power those challenges took on by the purpose they were given, which began with the perspective taken. Only I, the one who lives through those cycles, is able to allow for the space where truth can reveal it's self and power can emerge in the experience.

Power is within each of us. We already are all we need to be, is truth. However, power only has the life to breathe in our lives when given the space to emerge and the nourishment to grow. Engaging in a cycle that creates powerful living begins with being clear on the process of the motion of that cycle.

Motion moves. It moves things into and out of the space you are. We've already established that the space of you already has all the power you need, which also technically means you are already in the "space" you need to be in.

Without getting into the science of space; what is, is, and what "isn't, isn't". Truth operates as an absolute, even as it applies

to "time and space". They are what they
are, and that's only a measurement in order
for our human minds to comprehend the
infinite.

It's what clouds that "space" that needs to be moved.
Once all that covers the power is removed, the course
of pulling that which nourishes the power is next.

Clearing the space for power to emerge begins with
acceptance that the eyes I am looking into are my
own, whether or not they come in the mirrors that
generally hang on a wall. Whether or not they are the
hazel ones I know to be my own. If they are looking at
me, they are reflections.

Since the power is within me, so is that which covers
or clouds it. The mirrors have come to reflect back to
us a picture of what we are obviously not seeing within
ourselves. When we do not look within, the universe
will provide us a picture of them where we are looking.
Sometimes we are just standing too close to the
image to see it anywhere but from a distance around
us. Either way the universe will keep bringing them
back, reflections and images, until we choose to
perceive them, live through them and thus clear them.

Those reflections, or mirrors, ignite a perspective that
sets a course of power through our own choice. A
cycle that keeps turning and turning, creating more
and more of what it was fueled with. I created the
entirety of the stories I shared. What was shared was
my perspective of them in that moment. Further more,
what I share here, is still my perspective. What you
read, hear and interpret is your perspective. As my
perspectives of these stories shifted, so too, did the

power they had on me and the power I had in the situations.

I shared the continual turning of them to show you that just when you think you've reached the center of your onion, it keeps on bloomin'. My entire life has been one big blessing. I am abundant beyond what I know how to express in words, or even metaphors. And I still have challenges. They are not mutually exclusive. I stand in my power. Sometimes I forget, or become cloudy. I stand in front of the mirror, sometimes consciously, sometimes through another's eyes, to remind me. When I get there to look through eyes of my own, I live through it just the same. Release and Clear, Release and Clear.

Living powerfully is a practice, not a perfection, even though it's "perfect"! (smiles)

Thus to create a life of power, we must Be the power. The power we already are. Simply standing in your truth, in your power, brings about powerful living, a powerful life and a powerful you! The only way to get there is to live through the truth of your experiences, thus clearing the space covered by releasing illusions, continually revealing the truth in you. The power, the beauty, the abundance, that is the truth of you, has always been and is you.

Not that you became anything, that I became anything I wasn't before my marriage; before any of the experiences related here. I simply came to know, own, live and share that power through the process of living through them.

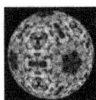

And the cycle keeps on churning. And the spaces keep getting bigger. The dusk begins to speak to you. Soon enough the light stops seeping in and simply surrounds you.

The stories and glimpses of my ever shifting kaleidoscope have been from my perspective.

We've all got a story. Some more dramatic than others. Some more "gifted" than others. Some more adventurous or mysterious. Our stories are the view we get from the lens of our scope, at the moment we are standing in them. We're always one moment, one shift, away from a completely different perspective, and story. Depending on which lens we view the same experience from, we might just get a different story from the same moment. Our own stories shift and shape as we move from moment to moment. The stories you read today might have been told different in the moment, different yet three years ago, and will certainly read different in five years or fifteen.

Learning how to create the experience of the view we have is the power I speak of.

> *"The point of power is in the present moment and in those moments we have a choice!" Uzuri*

These stories, this view from my scope, has been what I call my Cycle of Power . To a power I live today, solid in the grounding of who I am. That I already **am** all I need to be. And that 'ME', is the light of love.

That cycle still exists in full effect today. The work is still present, and the cycles of the seasons keep on turning. The harvest is a freedom and liberation of a gift I had no idea was behind the big red bow. Even so, what I write today as freedom will get redefined for me tomorrow as I keep unwrapping the gift, one moment at a time. What was thought to be a gift is actually just like that damn Bloomin' Onion. Only now it can be as inviting in my stomach as it appeared on the menu.

I've learned to know what I can eat, and what I have to let go. I learned that I can order more when I am hungry again. There's always more where that came from and sooner or later the waitress will come back around.

I still have days of smiles and sometimes nights of tears. Sometimes I am clear and others I am lost. Some days I remember, and others I forget. Sometimes I judge and others I accept. I always love in the various colors and shapes I am. How one experiences it, hears it, sees it and knows it depends on their shift of the lens. That goes for my reception of love from others as well.

I practice acceptance. I practice surrender. I find faith, when I lose my trust. I forgive when I find I am holding. I trust as I move along. One step at a time, I keep saying 'yes'. And although my cycles keep on churning, I am conscious today of whom I am. And who I am is who I've always been. I am love.

My process of power is not a becoming as it is a shedding, revealing more of her beauty every day. Today as I stand in front of that mirror I intimately know the eyes that look back at me. The softness they hold me with leaves a strength that's always available.

I have taken responsibility for me, owning my piece. I allow others the space to do the same. When I see a new place, an open space, where I can do more, I do. Where I can release more, I release.

I stand committed to my connection, living through the cycles of my power, peaceful and passionate, one choice at a time.

With an extended hand I share all that I am. Knowing we're only an extension of the source that connects us. More often than hear me, you'll see me live, "Mi casa es su casa!"

That mirror still shows up. With a new message every time, every once in a while one even repeats it's self. I have learned to love her, listen with more patience and experience with more grace. She's just the eyes of spirit looking back at me. And a little play goes a long way.

Considerations

I would like to take this time to reflect on the considerations. Again, there are many triggers within this book and it's non-spacial, shifty kind of style can leave us all a little dizzy, even when just reading it! Even if you've read it before, it will read different this time, so READ IT AGAIN PLEASE.

1. This is a non-spacial, shifty journey that's irreverent of "time". Get ready for an *Alice in Wonderland* expedition. That includes grammar that may, or may not, be typical or "proper". Remember in a time and space, where technically there is none, I ask you to release your limitations and allow yourself to simply flow moment to moment. Which may at times transition in ways that may not seem proper, typical or linear. Let it be what it is so it can take you where it needs to.

2. This story is not written in any chronological order. You will find yourself shifting from one point in life to another within in the story, which is kind of how our memories work when we get to the core. This story is organized in a flow of the message and encompassed in and around the feelings, which lead to the lessons and purpose of the experiences. This is ultimately the purpose of this book; to begin paying attention to the purpose, flowing with the process and pull back from the individual points in life to appreciate the individual moments more. Whenever you see a - shift. . .shift . . . . - you can certainly be guaranteed you are shifting. Most frequently that also means within the story and the timeline. It may be forward, it may be backward, it may be neither, but it's always a shift.

3. There are rabbit holes within rabbit holes. Understand this is not a one time catch all read. It's a bit like a Bloomin' Onion. The layers will keep on peeling, and peeling. Each time you read it, a new perspective will be present. With each new perspective another layer of wisdom will be revealed. Pick it up over and over again. Share it time and again. The wisdom it provides will cycle as you do. Keep on churnin'. . .

4. Triggers are buried within the pages, inside the stories, throughout the words and certainly contained in the truth. They were not necessarily intentional, but were certainly guided there. Those triggers will release a memory deep within you of a truth you've always known. Be aware of them. . . Some of them will trigger through love, others may trigger through fear. The feelings they evoke will be as vast and varied as the souls and personalities reading this book. Trust that the triggers, none-the-less, will bring you to a space of love and acceptance. They will bring you to the place of home.

5. Finally, honor yourself, as well as those around you as you cycle, and shift. Most of all, celebrate as you come on home.

Most of all take a moment to breathe before you continue. Even it its just 5 deep breaths. Set the book down for a moment, relax every muscle in your body, close your eyes and breathe.

The Point
of
Power

I took you through some of my cycles as a way to give you a point of reference.

In order to see where you want to be, you gotta know where you stand. To truly know my freedom, you've got to see my slavery, too. To be liberated you have to know the chains that bind you, own what got you there, and live through the process.

The point isn't the high or the low, but the consciousness of where we stand in relation to where we choose to be. As you begin to lose focus of the points, the highs and lows, and begin to focus in on the purpose, you'll, too, find yourself in the sometimes nauseating swirl. You'll also slip right into the space of liberation.

Consciousness of the process provides us that portal. The portal opens us to the unlimited power within. To create whatever world we choose. To liberation. To a place where time and space don't exist. To a place where what you think you create happens in an instant. To a place where only love exists. More importantly it gives us the strength to hold it in our days, our moments.

The portal to the liberation you seek begins with one simple, and yet voluminous shift.

One simple shift . . . One simple shift . . . and your whole world opens up. . .

"You already are all you need to be!"

Only in this space can you slip into the portal of truth.

The portal is wide and also specific. It is vast and also crystal clear. The liberation found in liberating yourself is the position of the portal prospect. You already are all you need to be!

Knowing, owning and living this one little truth allows you the space to resonate with the power that liberates you. The truth that is you. Resonating with it becomes a honing, as you realize the power of you that has always been.

Power is very simple and straight forward. The power within is projected out. The world around us acts as a mirror reflecting it back to us. Whenever we choose to know, or measure its effect, we simply need to look around us – results are the indicators.

It's simple science. As the energy thickens, mass is formed, thus manifestation. Even in simplistic addition $1+1=2$, $2+2=4$, $4+4=8$, and the growth builds exponentially upon it's self. What we are begins this course of motion. Getting to that core unleashes the liberation you bind within yourself.

Which leads me back to my original point; we already are all we need to be. Anything else clouds the situation. Getting to the core of you, the clarity of what "that" is, is the portal to the power that lies within us all. And the only thing blocking you is what you covered it with. Liberation is only found upon liberating you.

When the body has cancer it must be removed. If the cancer is not removed it builds upon it's self creating more cancer. You can cover it up. You can medicate it. You can mask it. You can teach it to do tricks.

Cancer is still cancer. Truth is still truth. Cancer still eats the body until there is nothing left to eat. The only way to stop it from eating the body is to remove the self destructive cells from the source of the food it feeds upon, your life.

You are life. And life, energy, by definition, is infinite. Only by getting to the core of its truth, the life within you, are you able to expand it.

"You already are all you need to be!"

Total acceptance of truth. Complete surrender to truth. Living the CORE of truth will free you to breathe its infinite liberation.

If it's not feeding you, it's eating you. Simply remove that which eats you. Reveal that which feeds you. The science [the spirit] will do the rest.

And, the cycles you just 'journeyed' through were all part of that process. The highs, the mid-points and the lows were all dispersed amongst each other. I chose to share more of the challenges, not only because I'd like you to shift your perspective, but more aptly shift your perspective in what often feels like the most "difficult" areas and times of our lives. It's often easier to shift during our joy, than during our challenges. I want you to see not only my joys and many, many blessings, but also the balance through the challenges and that this process lives and works not only in both ends of the spectrum but throughout the shades as well.

To walk the path when we see the pattern, to have a perspective of power when we're in the flow, is one thing. It's quite another to stand strong in the eye of the hurricane. It's the hurricane where most of us get swept away into the tunnels of chaos. We forget that the flow of the wind that swept us there has the same power to remove us from it. More important, the power that ignites the wind is the same power igniting us.

It was the moments of my storm, where I so often felt far away that I was closest to the truth. We will find ourselves in the middle of screaming, until we find the voice within to scream ourselves. And that which we see around us are only indications of the truth we have within.

I will say it again!!!

You already are all you need to be!

Total acceptance of truth. Complete surrender to truth. Living the CORE of truth will free you to breathe its infinite liberation. Sharing it with those around you applies the principles of math, creating exponential growth of that which you build upon.

If it's not feeding you, it's eating you. Simply remove that which eats you. Reveal that which feeds you. The science [the source] will do the rest.

The Point of Power

Power has great impact in our lives. Our ability to harness, and direct it, allows us to manifest our choices, to feel grounded, clear and strong. Our inability to harness or direct our power, our lack of clarity or perspective of our power, our misunderstanding of its dynamics and the natural inherent power we all have as an image of spirit can create a feeling and appearance of chaos. It can cause us to feel tired, stressed, and down right angry or rageful. It can create greed, jealousy, and egotistical vengeance, among many others.

On the other hand, a sense of our inherent power provides peace, balance and joy. It gives us a feeling of strength and grounding. It sheds light on the path of our choices, and the subsequent results we create, giving us the clarity we need to navigate through the space we are in comfortably, and with greater ease and joy. Ultimately it gives us a connection to the limitless love within us. Allowing us to regenerate our power from within, rather than turning to external, limited and unsubstantial power sources that end up taking more power than they generate.

When humans do not tap into their internal source of power they are left with the only other option there is. Search for that power around them. When one takes power from another to fill up themselves, they are not only draining that which they took it from, they are also expending exhorbinate amounts of energy to refuel via a limited source.

Imagine the time and energy it takes to find fuel from outside sources. To constantly drain them from the sources around us and then have to find new sources as the ones around us dry up or close off. Now imagine the energy and time it takes to sit still and allow a clear pipe connecting us to the limitless source of fuel, or power, flowing directly into us. The choice seems pretty simple.

When one knows, connects with and lives the power they are within themselves, they spend much less time looking for it around themselves. Among many things, this can reduce stress, fear, longing, confusion and fatigue. More importantly the clarity to which it flows directly to us creates stability, peace and increased energy! Our ability to influence it ourselves, in partnership with the spirit we are, increases our sense of safety and stability from within.

Power is simply an active state of wisdom, spirit alive within us. We take information and transform it into knowledge when we internalize that information, giving it meaning to us. We create wisdom when we integrate that knowledge with spirit. Power is the enaction of that wisdom, the living energy it takes on in our lives.

The clarity of our power, and the enaction of it in our lives, can create a state of limitlessness, utter liberation, regardless of external circumstances. The connection to power, as used in this reference, is simply the point of integration with spirit, as you know it. I will use the words for spirit in this text to refer to spirit as I know it and allow for a universal openness to application. You can at any time replace that word with any reference you choose. The point of this text is not the word, or the way in which you connect to it. The point is the power gained from the integration and the cycle one goes through to get there. Even those who have no "spiritual" practice can apply this principle in the same manner.

The Process

The inherent nature of infinite power is a process, rather than a destination. So no matter where you are, if you choose to know the power of "you" at a greater depth, the process, and the results, will be the same. There is no "there". If you think you are "there" you certainly are not. Power is a process of expansion and liberation, a continuous cycle; with no beginning and no ending just like a circle. Because it's infinite you can continue to enjoy the miracles and joy it provides in every area, at every time in your life. The only thing that can limit you, is you. Commitment, openness and trust in the process are all you need.

A Principle of Truth:
This entire principle of power is based on two truths,
1: Power is limitless.
2: You have unlimited access to that power.

The process is universal and cyclical. It doesn't matter who you are or where you are in life. Only a belief that you "already know" will limit its wisdom.

This process of connecting to the already available and alive power within you is the same for the alcoholic, as it is for the corporate executive. It is the same for a man, as it is a woman. It is the same for a child, as it is the elders. It is the same for the sad, and the joyful, the playful and the aggressive. The process and the subsequent results are all the same.

The choice is yours. In life there are two cycles to partake in. Both are cyclical. Both inherently build on each other. At every moment we are given choices and those choices determine where we go next, the experiences we have and the results we realize.

The process goes a little like this:

- What we perceive determines what we believe.
- What we believe forms the choices we make.
- The choices we make lead to the action we take.
- The action we take produces the results we experience.

Those results either reinforce the original perspective or they provide a space for a new perspective to arise. Thus goes the cycle.

We are either conscious of that process or we are not. When we are conscious of that cycle we are able to influence the various points within that cycle. We have a sense of our power in that cycle and understand how to harness and direct it in manners that create the results we choose to experience. We are able to do so with greater ease and comfort.

When we are not conscious of that cycle we are "victim" to its turning, its process and its results. We expend great amounts of energy, feeling fatigued, frustrated, confused and lost. Like the drowning body, our spirits begin to gasp for air and reach for anything around us that can keep us breathing.

In order to experience liberation, we must tap into our inherent, infinite source of power. To affect the results of our choices, and do so with comfort and ease, we must become conscious of what I call the Cycle of Power .

We must go through a four stage process; Know, Own, Live and Share our power.

The Cycle of Power

This is the Cycle of Power. The cycle we can engage in that will turn our "knowing" into an active state of living. The cycle, that with clarity of it, will lend way to a space that allows us to influence our results and the experiences we have in life. Moreover, to do so with ease and comfort.

Most people think consciousness is this grand gift that provides immediate relief from suffering, allowing abundance, health and peace to amass in one's life. I am here to say that is not necessarily so. There are no instant rewards, or 'quick cash' as they may say. Just when you think you've arrived you could feel like you're falling again. But whether or not you're falling, or climbing, or resting in between, more often than not, depends on the view from where you are standing.

It's all perspective. There in lies the power. As you move to the center of the cycle the point of perspective becomes clearer, the perspective of the points churn, and the truth emerges. The experience of which is only experience.

No matter where we are in the on-going cycle, on the points, in the center, or anywhere in between, there is a deep sense of power we can live, allowing us to live love and joy along the path. Understanding, in the Cycle of Power , is the first step in getting there. Making the choice to consciously dive right in is all yours, as it was mine.

Conscious living is a process of engaging in the Cycle of Power. So let's first go over what the Cycle of Power is.

The Cycle of Power is a "new" perspective of a constant truth. Below you will see the graphic of the cycle:

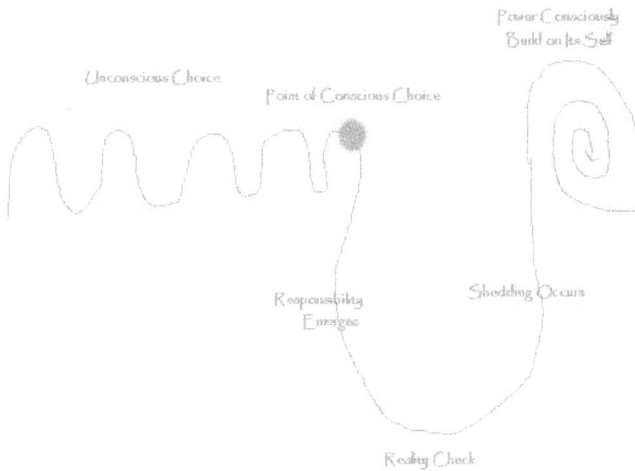

Power Consciously Build on Its Self

Unconscious Choice

Point of Conscious Choice

Responsibility Emerges

Shedding Occurs

Reality Check

You will notice on the left hand side of the page is unconscious choice. This is where most people live. They experience highs and lows, high and lows, highs and lows, throughout life. In actuality those highs and lows indicated are actually cycles beginning and ending, then opening into another cycle. Without consciousness, though, they appear and feel like highs and lows, highs and lows.

For example, the cocaine addict who sniffs his white powder in order to feel high, only to experience an extreme low, needing that high again. Or the sugar high given when we eat a snickers for lunch, coffee for breakfast or soda at night getting a quick high, only to experience the sugar low that comes a few hours later, requiring another quick high to sustain our bodies. Or even the seminar or self-help junkie who comes out of a workshop pumped up, high on life, only to return to work on Monday and wonder where all that energy went.

These cycles offer us opportunities to make conscious choice creating conscious results at each high and low. However, unconscious choice keeps people in the experience of highs and lows that seem to happen randomly. People on this side of the cycle experience high levels of fatigue, stress and pain as they attempt to find higher highs, and fewer lows.

You then come to the middle of the cycle, called the 'Point of Conscious Choice'. This is kind of like the movie, *The Matrix*. You get to choose the red pill or the blue pill. Once you take it, there is no turning back. It can be a rocky road at points, even long for some. For some it may feel like falling into the rabbit hole. However, peace, power and passion are promises at the end of that road, and often along the journey home.

On the graphic, you'll notice as you "fall" down the hill we call this 'Responsibility'. It is shown as a fall because of how it often feels to most people. The point at the bottom of that hill is called a 'Reality Check'.

Let's use this example, you just graduated from college and have $50,000 in debt. You make $50,000 a year. You realize that this income is not going to pay down your debt. In order to get on solid ground and begin to gain abundance you need to earn more. So you take responsibility for that debt by getting a job making twice what you are earning now. You begin making $100,000. You get an immediate rush. Woo Hoo! You can buy a house, get a Range Rover, maybe a bit of bling bling!

Then "reality" sets in. You have $50,000 in debt still. The responsibility emerges, and the cash goes out the door as fast as it comes in. You actually feel a lower low than you ever had. You are working harder, being more responsible and yet have the same or less than before. What happened? You begin to feel like this consciousness stuff is for the birds! Ignorance is bliss right?!!

It's called a reckoning with truth. Until you stand in the face of it, it's not really responsibility. Only in the responsibility does the release occur.

At the point of reality, shedding begins to occur, as you'll notice on the up swing of the falling hill above. Consciousness requires that you clean house. Depending on how much or how long you have been unconscious. Depending on how much you are covered and how deep you are cloaked determines how long and hard that shedding process is. Where you get stuck in the process depends on you and your experience, perspective and beliefs.

"Climbing" back out of that rabbit hole is a shedding process, noted on the right hand side of that dip.

Kaleidoscope   189

Growth, or what we call expansion, is a shedding process, rather than an adding process. You have to unlearn everything you were taught in order to remember all that you already know!

Let me repeat that. **You have to unlearn everything you were taught in order to remember all that you already know!**

You already are all you need to be. You are powerful. You are peaceful. You are passionate. You are all you need to be right now. You are pure light. Shedding is the process of releasing all that covers your light.

This is often a hard process for most people. It's the part of the road where resistance can be strong. This is the part of the road where the fabric with which you've stood for so long begins to unravel. Where the walls you built and the lines you drew fade away. Where the things you thought were protecting you have no precedence anymore. Although, it's making way for the freedom found in flying, it often feels like the bottom just fell out of your safety net and you're free falling to death.

You mean all I have to do is shed everything that is covering my power? You mean I already am powerful? I already am all I need to be? I have been powerful all along? You mean I was running in a hamster wheel this whole time? You mean I created all that pain myself? You mean I don't need this or that? I don't have to be this or that? You mean all those should be this and should do that, should have all this were all phasads I gave undo merit?

All that felt solid will now begin to feel fluid and those who are use to walking find floating a bit nauseous! And the faster and harder you were running the more harsh the shift to floating with feel. Have faith. Remember commitment, openness and trust in the process are all you need.

They say insanity is simply doing the same thing over and over again while expecting a different result. So take the leap to a new space and trust that it will deliver a new result. If it wasn't getting you there before it's not likely to now either. If it wasn't all that grounding before, it's probably not solid. And although it feels like you are falling, remember there are no limits here so there is no landing. Surrender to it and find your wings, it's quite easy to turn the falling into flying in a space that's wide open, with nowhere to land, and everywhere to go!

As you emerge from the shedding you begin to see all that already is. It's called the Cycle of Power ! You can see the entire process. You have the power in the palm of your hands!

You perceive
You believe
You choose
You act
You experience [Results]

Notice in the graph that this is a cycle. In a cycle there is a high point, a mid-point, a low point and another mid point before you reach another high point again. Life is not all bliss. Consciousness is not perfection, it's perspective. Abundance is not mutually exclusive from "loss". The contradictions are just perspectives themselves, ones that lead to experiences that lead to perspectives and it all keeps churning.

Sure things are not "perfect". They are in divine order. And more importantly you are able to clearly see and move through what appears to be or feels like pain with ease and comfort, knowing that it is truly light, and love. There is acceptance, rather than attachment. It's called the Cycle of Power ! Welcome to it.

Acceptance and Connection

Acceptance only comes through connection, which requires the release of attachment.

You'll notice a very key point, in the perspective of power, is that surrounding attachment and connection.

The Cycle of Power requires connection in the most pure and whole sense you can possibly muster up. It also requires an absolute release of attachment.

The left side of the cycle is all about attachment. The right side of the cycle, where the cycle comes into full focus, occurs through connection.

Attachment is very different than connection. And more importantly a lack of attachment doesn't necessarily equate to detachment. Anytime you are in attachment you are out of truth.

Let's take a quick look at each. Attachment is static. It claims a destination, an end. I am attached to an outcome, for example. I experience highs and lows simply because I focus, am attached to the points, the ends, the destinations. Attachment also equates a hold. It's a holding of something, often anything. It generally occurs because there is a perception of separation. I see only the high and the low, no connection of the two, but rather a separation; one high and one low, one right, the other wrong, one good, the other bad.

Naturally where there is connection, there is no need to hold. Where there is wholeness there is flow. With no beginning and end in wholeness there is no destination, only a flow from one to another, onto another.

Attachment is a clear indicator you are out of the cycle, no longer standing in the truth. A cycle is a flow and anything contradicting it will pull you right out of it. The removal from it, the truth, is as immediate as the connection can be to it. They are both states of absolution, on opposite sides of the pole. One of truth, the other of fear.

You can be in the middle of the Cycle of Power and as soon as you found yourself there can pull yourself right back out by attaching. It literally sucks the life, the power right out of the situation, the relationship, you name it.

Any time you are in anything static, attached, holding, or with an ending, or destination you are out of truth. The power just seeps right out.

Connection, on the other hand, is integration. It maintains healthy boundaries that are malleable, clear and consistent. Connection requires wholeness. In order for one to connect to another there has to be one in the first place, and another in the second place.

Connection sees the process, rather than the destination. It connects to the purpose at the core, rather than the points along the path. Thus you find yourself on the right side of the cycle when in connection.

An indicator of attachment is emotion. Emotion is a reaction, a response. It is a doing unto; which means you were static enough for something to happen "to" you, so you can respond back to it.

On the other hand, feeling is a state of being. It is an extension of our connection, the expression of our experience. It is a flow.

Emotion: static: powerless! Feeling: dynamic: powerful!

If you are in the middle of emotion, look keenly around and soon enough you will find the associated attachment. Release the attachment, accept the truth, surrender to the process, open to the truth and connect to the source.

You move that quickly in and out of your own power.

Practice, Practice, Practice. . . .

Moment to moment and instant to instant you can claim or relinquish your power. Then what keeps you in it?

Practice.

Life is a living. You gotta do it.

You perceive.
You believe.
You choose.
You act.
You experience.

Every one of those is a flow, an action. They are a living. To stay in the power of life you simply need to keep practicing.

Practice. Practice. Practice.

You don't need any answers. You simply need to remain connected and flow. Just say 'yes', remember. Spirit will do the rest.

The more you do it. The more it becomes you. A commitment to action becomes a practice. Because even a choice is an action, that perpetuates movement that builds upon it's self. Soon enough a practice becomes a living.

A Little Elbow Grease

"It takes a little elbow grease," as my mother would say. There is no easy solution or answer to getting there. "You got yourself in, you're gonna have to dig your way out," she'd say. You learn the truth of your mother's words upon becoming a mother. It's like this download that happens upon birth, and continues to assimilate as your own children grow.

I earned my elbow grease the good old fashion way. My mother's bath tub still probably has the rings of mud to prove it. People laugh when they hear how I pulled weeds taller than I at 7 years old and picked up rocks in a gravel barn yard. Yes it's true. I grew up on a farm and I really did those things.

My grandfather told the age-old stories of walking up hill both ways to school, in the snow with no shoes. It was true for him. [Winks] My mother even had an outhouse and went to a one-room school house for grammar school. Talk about understanding work ethic. Yes we live in this century.

The good old farm life teaches you a thing or two about being responsible, though. You actually grow your food. In fact, we grow food for part of the world. My brother got up each morning to complete his morning chores before school. And it wasn't cleaning his room, or taking out the garbage. Those were the afternoon chores. He had to feed the cattle, the dogs and check the fences. I was gathering eggs in the chicken coop! The weekend jobs were things like building fence, bailing hay, shucking corn, canning vegetables. You get the picture.

I hated the farm when I was a little girl. The city has been calling me for years. I will always be a city girl at heart, hearing her hum in my ear. But the farm is ground into my soul. It's the foundation on which I could understand the value of the city and the gifts of life it's self. You see all those people eat what we cultivated on the farm. The seeds they know as blooms began on that farm. However, we actually had to till the ground we planted and harvest the seeds we sowed. Doing so with Mother Earth taught me how to do so in my life.

The life I have led makes the life I am in now seem even sillier. You see on the farm you don't get a good harvest unless you actually plant the seeds. If they aren't planted in fertile soil with well-tilled land they've got a rocky start, literally. You need to spend the summer nourishing the plants that are growing, and then harvest them in the fall.

In today's world that's a very, very simplistic understanding of the farming industry. My father spends time understanding the market trends. Buys all this fancy, smancy equipment. Watches the weather channel every night. He even has Doppler radar in his thousand[s] square foot office to run his 3500 acre farm.

But most of all, he did a lot of surrendering. He understood once he tilled the ground, planted the seeds, and nourished the plants the rest was up to mother nature. If he did the work he would harvest the grain. "Take care of her and she takes care of you." He said.

During those summers of waiting for the grain to grow my grandfather used to drive the fields. He used to have this old silver pick-up, rusted out and filled with boxes of Pall Mals. The smell of it nauseated me. The ten miles an hour he drove were a bit frustrating. But sitting with my Pa was worth it. And in the early summer, if I was really good, we could stop at the railroad tracks and pick the juniper flowers blooming. He spent hours telling me these stories that made no sense to me. I used to roll my eyes and wonder when they would be over. Today I wish I could remember what they were! I know there was wisdom in those long, slow drives and stories that felt the same.

You see I've learned by driving from field to field that one field next to another can garner very different yields. So, in order to get results you need to do the work and then leave the rest to Mother Nature. It may begin with the soil, but someone is responsible for tilling that land. And year after year the yield it produces is based largely on the way it was treated.

Even further, no one can truly teach you how to yield a good harvest. Much of it is learned in the relationship you garner with mother earth. By listening to her when she speaks and working hand-in-hand with her season after season.

I watched my father for years. Always wondering how he was such a successful farmer with so many farms going under around him. With all his harshness, he was most of all a hard worker. And best of all, a man with a great ability to lead people and follow mother earth. I used to ask, "How do you know dad? How do you know when to plant, when to harvest, when and how much to sell?"

He said, "You just know Shannon, you just know."

When I used to be lost in my intellect I thought he was crazy. There must be a formula to this I said. And after 30+ years of being a successful farmer he ought to know it by now! Now I know better.

Sure Grandpa taught him a few things. And he is now teaching my brother. The knowledge they teach though is mostly in the machines, the tools they use. However, the wisdom they have gained is from the hard work they have done. Working the land year after, year. That isn't taught. It's lived.

So when people asked me to write a book, as they have been doing for years. When they asked me to share my wisdom I laughed. I thought how do you put that in a book? More importantly, is it all that wise to write a book telling people not to read a book, but to live life!? 'Cuz that's about all I get typed on the first page before it all seems a little absurd to me. You can't teach people how to live life, especially not in a book.

My grandmother is still asking me what I do, ten years later. I told her "I guide people to their inner purpose in life. I give them the tools to create what they choose in life." She gave me the most quizzical look. "Don't people just know that?" She said. She is wiser than she knows.

What seemed so obvious to her. Seems so obscure to others. To her planting in the Spring and harvesting in the Fall is the cycle of life. Most people these days walk on concrete, though. They don't even feel the dirt beneath their feet, let alone plant seeds in it. And we wonder why we don't know how to grow blossoms in our life.

Teaching people how to yield a harvest in their life is no more taught than that relationship my father has with Mother Earth after 35 years of farming and three generations of intuition passed along in the genes. You see yields in life, results, are experienced. They take as much work and nourishment as every plant that grows in the ground Mother Earth provides us. It takes just as much work, and just as strong of a connection with her, as my father has, to yield his crops.

So as I have sat down to write this book, as with all the others that ended up in the trash can, I thought: "How do you write a book to tell everyone not to read a book because it has no answers? How do you produce a seminar so that everyone can learn they already have all the answers?" Seems a little ironic to spend a day showing people they already have all the answers, and most of all they don't need to learn anything new or become anything other than what they already are.

"Now, that will be $5000 please!"

That quizzical look from my grandmother just creeps up every time. "Oh no, Shannon." She says, "They don't really pay you for that. Do they? How much did you say?" She must think I am really selling drugs. Maybe she thinks I am on them myself. Sometimes I think they are too, Grandma!

By living in the city now, I understand why. They never had to sow their blooms, or even plant their seeds. They bought them down the street at the corner market. The smart ones get them straight from the growers at the weekly farmers market. Those too busy to bother spend the extra money to get it on the street corner from the person who bought from the grower at last week's farmer's market. And the farmer is taking his cash, and more importantly his wisdom, home, while the man on the street is taking his blooms to his house.

Obviously I am writing a book. So what did I realize? You only learn through experience. This is the truth. Still the truth. Always the truth. Even gurus in Tao, Buddhism and all the masters in centuries old philosophies, Jesus himself, knew what my grandfather knew. You can impart wisdom one of two ways:

Story. . .
Through stories passed on from generation to generation. There was nothing new in my grandfather's stories. They might as well have been the ones chiefs told years ago in teepees. They were just told in his experience, in his language. You see, in stories one can garner a morsel of wisdom through the experience of another. It's done by gaining a new perspective that you can transfer into visualized experience. Ultimately it's just a trigger, shifting your kaleidoscope to an experience you've already had or bringing you a new experience altogether, based on the shift in perspective.

That leads to experience. . . .

The other method of gaining wisdom is through good old experience it's self. In the end, even if you gained perspective through story, you will still need to do the work to gain the result of the wisdom. There is no getting around the work. Harvest doesn't happen until after the work of Spring, and the patience found in Summer's wait. Beautiful thing is, it's always guaranteed to be followed by the hibernation and rest of Winter before Spring returns again!

Now I know what my grandfather really meant when he said, "finish your work before you play, only hard work garners fun play." I spent my twenties thinking he was so old school. It was about working smarter, not harder. I now know we are both wise. They are not mutually exclusive. And work really wasn't what I thought it was. Wish he had told me that! Working smart can sometimes be hard work too. And working hard doesn't always mean you weren't smart about it. More over, you can play through the process, or find joy in it all. It's a lot of responsibility being accountable to that relationship we have with our partner, the universe. Or in farming, often referred to as the Earth. There is no smart work without a solid relationship with that partner!

It's how my father does so well with a farm so large in a territory where more farmers are loosing their ass than the pounds within it! There is just no getting around the tilling of the soil, the planting of the seeds and the nourishing of the growth. There is no getting around the surrender found in Summer. It all leads to the fruits of Winter!

So how does a book give you experience when it is gained in the living you are not doing while reading this book? Back to the irony, right! Because we both know now that you're gonna have to do the work either way. And more importantly the work you do depends on the land you're living on.

In fact, I live in Vegas now. I lived in San Diego for ten years and the rest of my wonderful existence was in Illinois. First of all, the growing seasons all vary. The soil differs, the climate shifts are diverse and the blooms they best cater to are separate. So when I would call my father, while trying to plant a garden in my San Diego back yard [Which at the time was technically a tarp covering my cement 'backyard', lined with brick to hold the soil in a 2 inch garden!] he had no idea when to tell me to plant, when they would sprout and when they'd be ripe. I thought, "See, I knew it, fathers don't know everything! Not even what they spent 35 years doing! What good is that?"

Ah, they are right, experience does impact wisdom. Along the way I figured out that was because he could only work with what he had a relationship with, a connection to. And it wasn't the land in San Diego, certainly not my soil filled box on concrete. He understood the tools of the trade. He learned them from my grandfather and is teaching them to my brother. He knew to tell me that I had to till the ground, or in my case the earth filled box. He knew to tell me how this pesticide would kill everything and that one might only kill this or that. He knew what tools I could leave on the shelf and which ones I couldn't do without.

So it came to me while sitting here wondering how to tell you that life experience will only give you the wisdom you need. It came to me while figuring out how to finesse the story, "You already have all the answers. You already are all you need to be!"

How do I know the answers? How did my parents, a mother who grew up with an out-house and a father who couldn't answer how he harvested such good yields, instill it in me without ever telling me? How did my brother and I become such responsible, accountable people, of such fine character in a world so devoid of such? How did my grandmother living a simple life in the middle of what appeared to be nowhere know so much more than all those people with all that information at their finger-tips?

I had an instant vision of those damn weeds at least two feet taller than I. My father yelling at two kids hardly old enough to spell to "pull them out of the grain bins", where no one went anyway I thought! I had a vision of my brother and I picking up rocks in a gravel barn yard in those humid summers that were summer vacation to every other child. What made no sense to me then, made lightening sense to me now.

Maybe they didn't know it. Maybe it's all they knew. But generation, after generation, of farmers, hunters and gathers have worked in direct connection with the very land that provides them the sustenance to live on. In that very experience of living, planting, harvesting, and eating so they can do it all over again next year, they know how to live by simply living. They produce the yield based both on the integration and connection they have to the land they are planting on and the work they put into it. Learning how to live just makes no sense to them. It's just something you do. The results are simply the experience, or manifestation, of the life they lead. Now, even the dumb-founded look on my family's face when I tell them what I do makes ALL the sense in the world. I call these 'monk moments'.

I feel like those funny little monks who sit around laughing all day at seemingly random events that make no sense to some folks. Yet make divine sense to them. Even that makes me laugh! The simplicity of life. The irony of it all. It's like watching cats chase their tails. And we all know what herding cats is like! It's why farmers raise cattle.

Doing the Work

We've all watched *Karate Kid*, right? Wax on, Wax off. Before enlightenment; wax on, wax off. After enlightenment; wax on, wax off!

The connection is really up to you; moving from unconscious choice to conscious choice, from a 'forgetting' of power to an engaging in power. Wax on, wax off, wax on, wax off. Just do the work. And most importantly no matter which side you are on, keep doing the work. Commitment, openness and trust in the process is all you need. And you'll never stop needing it no matter where you are. Keep working the ground and the ground will work. The plants will grow and the fruits will provide. The Winter will come and the plants will die. The Spring will return and fruit will grow again. Just keep working the ground. The plants will grow and the fruits will provide.

Like my dad said, "You just have to work the ground Shannon and see for yourself. I don't live in San Diego." A lot of help I thought that was. If I only knew how much help that was!! When you do the work you will know the connection.

You see we can trigger a memory of it. We can be examples of it. We can provide you the space to move into it, and the opportunity to experience it through our own stories. We can give you the tools to work your own ground with. But in the end you are the one standing on the land. You are the one who knows what you want to yield. You will have to be the one to plant the seed and harvest the land.

One of the best lessons I ever learned from my father, quite unknowingly by the way, was that Summer is the most important part of the yield. When I thought he was doing nothing and my grandfather was driving around aimlessly, and by the way slowly, doing nothing. They were really listening to the earth, watching the signs and surrendering to the process. This was the time for Mother Earth to do her part. This was the lesson of connection!

Shh! Listen!

So may you find the wisdom you have within. May you find the way to the source of power you have at your own core. May you be inspired to find the courage to surrender to that source. It can be a journey up hill both ways, sometimes in the snow and often without shoes! At the top of that hill, though, is a school. It's often one room and built on the earth. There are lots of windows where the wind whirls through and the sun shines in. It's called your body and it came to earth as a seed planted, that blossomed into you.

Remember, you don't have to teach a plant to grow. It grows toward the sunlight without you telling it to do so. It drinks the rain when it falls upon it. All a plant needs to grow is the space to emerge from the soil and the nourishment Mother-Nature already provides, at just the right time.

Think about it. Imagine five plants placed in row, on a window ledge. The first one has a blue ribbon on it. It's the champion of plants. The second one has a title listed on it. It's the CEO and President of all plants. The third one has lots of money, gold chains and bling bling all around it. The fourth plant comes equipped with a cheerleader, and lots of motivation. The fifth and final plant is just a plain plant. Which one will grow faster and larger?

They will all grow regardless of their external factors. In fact, the plain plant may grow faster and larger because it's not obstructed from the sun light, water and space it needs to emerge from the soil. In the end, they'll all grow.

You don't need to teach a plant to grow. It naturally moves toward the sunlight, soaks up the water and emerges from the space it's provided in the soil it lives in.

These stories have been sent to trigger a memory in you. The memory found deep within, that when raised to the surface, brings with it the very consistency of the source it's self.

You see the source is the answer to everything. A connection to the source of life is all that plant needs to grow. Just like you. And just like that plant the source of life is found within.

A friend of mine said to a business partner and I in a meeting recently that his next book was going to be 800 pages. On each page would be one line, "Go to the Source." He would sell it as the wisest book you've ever read; containing the answers to every question you ever had. Anytime you had a question you could ask the question and open to a page that would provide the precise and accurate answer, each and every time. Simple and straightforward.

"What more do you tell someone?" He asked "It's all there is. Go to the Source!"

People write books, pages upon pages, that all tell you the same thing in five hundred different ways. You're almost to the end of one! Our bookstores and libraries are filled with them. Why not just tell them, "Go to the Source!"

My business partner suggested that it include a chapter for each type of person. The chapter for Christians would say, "Go To God". The chapter for Muslims, "Go To Allah". The chapter for New Agers, "Go To The Light." Anytime you had a challenge in life you could open the book and it would give you the accurate advice for that challenge, Go To Source! Simple, absolute truth!

The irony for me is that we are the source, a manifestation of "it". You already are all you need to be. The power of you lies within you. It IS you. It doesn't actually take going anywhere, or doing anything. It takes standing still, listening, and surrendering to the connection. The sun shines on us naturally. We simply have to drink the rain as it falls and keep our space clear so we can emerge from the soil.

Our connection to this source, our integration with our Center, creates all that we experience in the world around us. In order to create consciously we must integrate with the very center of our being, the source. Conscious choice creates conscious results. The consciousness of your personal Core, your truth, is your wand, your Abra Cadabra, your pixie dust. The power to create lies within you. You are the magician.

Because you are the absolute manifestation of the source. Pull out your wand, say your Abra Cadabra and watch the Pixie Dust fly!

The results we experience in our lives, from hard results like money, jobs, and relationships to softer results, like harmony, balance, and joy, are all expressions of the wand we swung! It began with the perspective we had that formed the belief we hold. That led to the choices we made, the actions we took and the results we experienced.

As dad and grandpa always said, "keep working the ground." What they always said, never through words, was that working that ground kept you connected to it; connected to the source of that which produced the harvest of your seeds.

When we ARE the very source, we realize this is where it all resides. The source, now synonymous with ourselves, already is all it needs to be. It doesn't need to be taught. It doesn't need to be taller, shorter, fatter or thinner. It doesn't need credentials, a title, a fatter pay check, a cheer leader or even a little bling bling. Paying that $5000 to learn what you already knew now becomes silly. Paying $5000 to realize you didn't need to do anything or become something now becomes ironic. The gratefulness for the opportunity to remember is priceless!

It's just simple, straight-forward truth. Free of any religion, philosophy or politics. Truth. The kind you learn by farming the land we live on and harvesting the food we nourish our bodies with. The kind that remains the same, eyes open or closed. Truth. Simple, straightforward truth.

For us it's like plugging a light into a socket. It automatically turns on. And the light it shines into a dark room can at first be blinding, but at last provides crystal clarity about things you didn't even know to ask before. All it needed was an awareness of our inherent connection to the source.

In Closing

Loss.

I just kept losing. Or did I? "Losing." Losing, until I lost enough of myself that I found all I had always been.

Spinning.

I just kept spinning. Spinning, until I was moving so fast that everything around me began to stand still. Still. I just stood still; dazed in the loss of the spin, and the spin of the loss.

Stripped.

Stripped to the core. Naked. Standing still in that moment I found courage wrapping herself around me in ways I had no idea she could hold.

In our moments. In our moments of pain, drenched in the feeling of loss, drowning in our own tears, shedding the layers that have for so long covered us we begin to find a space. A space to stand. A space we call home.

And in our moments of Joy. Until we find ourselves dancing. Dancing in the middle of a crowd. There too, shedding the layers that have for so long covered us, we begin to find a space. A space to stand. A space we call home.

Lost.

Get lost in the flow of the music.

Feel the bass in your bones. Let your blood flow with
the harmony, and the melody take you to mediation.
Flow. Your entire body flows to the music. The music
that begins in your ears and moves to your muscles.
Move. Move to the music. Dancing in the dominion of
your soul.

The seeds you plant grow into the fruits you eat. And
when you get tired of continuously shaking the
branches dropping the dead fruit to the ground below.
. .

You just gotta pull up the tree, roots and all.

And you wonder what you'll do without the shade of
that tree; the tree that has provided so much shade
and shelter over the years.

Now, the light without that tree seems so bright. It's
blinding at first. And hot. So very hot. The shade. . .
Where's the shade of that tree? Curled up in the heat,
even the stench of that rotten fruit is worth the shade
of that tree. Rocking back and forth, curled up; back
and forth.

With your eyes closed, you become sensitive to
sound. The sound of the space you've found yourself
in. Still curled up, your body begins to move to the
sweet sound. As Bouble whales, "Let me go home, let
me go home, I've had my run, baby I'm done, let me
go home. . . mmmm."

"Surrounded by a million people, I will still be all alone."

And the melody takes you. The wind picks up and the tears fall like a rain storm in southeast Asia. Falling, and falling, and cleansing.

In the middle of a million people and my body rocks and rocks. . . Dancing to the music in my soul.

Found. It was me. That blinding light. It is me. The beauty. It was me all along. The wind whipping around me, swirling, and swirling. It's me. It's so beautiful.

Home.

I'm Home.

[Deep breath. Very, very deep breath.]

Opening my eyes, still dancing in the wide open space where that tree once grew; with little more than a seed in the palm of my hand. And the light still shines as it begins to set.

Dusk.

Dusk begins to arrive.

Her hazy hues, a smell so moist my lips are wet.

Standing in her crossroads. When the sun is half down, and then just on the other side of the horizon. The night has yet to fall, though you can feel the depth of it approaching. The lightness of the day is waning, and yet you can still feel the inspiration of its light.

Dusk.

It's the moment of the day when we are gifted the opportunity of reflection and foresight, all at once. The silence of it fills me even when I pay it no attention. Gratefulness absorbs me.

Digging my toes in the sand below, making a home for the seed in the palm of my hand. The seed of the fruit I wish to reap. Reap with the wisdom I have today, full of the faith that as it blooms the layers will peel themselves back revealing yet another seed, leaving me only truth.

And seed after seed, I am here to spread my fruit. The fruit I am at the point of the seed, nourished with the tears of my shedding as the roots take grounding in the floor of Mother Earth, spreading her branches into the space of the light that rises and falls; from one dusk to another.

And the blooms keep on bloomin'. . . The shifts keep on shiftin'. . .

At the end of the day, it doesn't matter where we are, 'who' we are, what we are doing, where we are doing it, or who we are doing it with. . . We are who we are. Who I was in each of those moments, in each of those relationships, was me. My power shone through, moment to moment, regardless of whether or not I recognized it.

This applies to everyone. We are who we are, regardless. Our truth lives whether or not we are conscious of it. The patterns in our life are the indicators of our 'nature'. As we become conscious of those patterns, the indicators of the truth. As we begin to know them, own them, live them and share them, we get to harness the power of them, to gleam the joy from them.

Those patterns, the indicators, are also what some may call the proof in the pudding. If we stop for just a moment to think about what it is we are generally doing, where we generally find ourselves, who we are generally 'being' in relation to, both the people and the world around us, the indicators of our truth, and thus truth it's self, would begin to peer around the veil at us.

I was having dinner with a client recently. I was listening to him share a little about his truth, without him knowing he was doing so. He told me how his wife said he was either a shit magnet or a guardian angel.

He is an assistant Chief in one of our national 'responder' agencies. In fact, he has worked as a responder most of his life. He is an EMT as well. He's also a bit of an adventurer. A quote from him says it all:

"I'm going with the cram as much fun and adventure into this [life] -- bull riding and chasing Mexican drug cartels through the desert on 4 wheelers are a couple of the more adventurous [*stories*] (that I mention in polite company anyway). 'Life is not a journey to the grave with the intention of arriving safely in a pretty and well preserved body, but rather to skid in broadside, thoroughly used up, totally worn out and loudly proclaiming - 'Wow, what a ride' ".

So I asked, "What do you mean shit magnet or guardian angel?"

He proceeds to share with me a few examples that sum up his existence. Essentially, major disasters occur in front of him all the time. They happen in extreme settings, without the typical tools to respond available. He hasn't gone on a vacation without this happening. They range from a man having a heart attack on a volcano, to major car crashes and children being severely burned in the middle of national parks. You name it he's there when it happens.

In fact, in the last example of the burn victim in a national park, a gentleman stopped by. He stated he was a doctor and asked if he could help with the child who'd been severely burned. My client turned to the gentleman and said, "I appreciate your offer sir, but unless you are a burn specialist with all the tools that come with that specialty, there's not much more you can do." The gentleman gleamed, "Well I am. In fact, I have a trunk in my car where I always carry the 'tools' I might need in emergencies just like these!"

I smiled and said, "Wow, thank you for sharing that with me. It's so inspiring to hear stories of people living their truth so vigorously! You do realize, you're there, with those people, at that moment, because that's just who you are, right?!"

He smiled and said, "I guess. I never really thought about it like that."

Now granted I hear stories like this daily, because of course that's what I do! In addition, responders, and similar industries, are easy examples given their passionate, service oriented nature. But this story, this truth, applies to each and every single one of us, exactly the same!

He's a great example of how we all live our truth regardless of titles, positions, limitations, boxes, jobs, relationships, 'time' and location. We are who we are in every situation, in every environment, in every moment we live; even when we are not aware of it.

I explained to him that's just what he is here to do, it's who he is. He shared a common feeling: "What happens when I complete that? Does that mean it's all over!?"

I laughed and explained, "It's a process; living our truth that is. That's just what life is. There is no end or beginning. We are who we are regardless of whether or not we are conscious of it. We do it consistently regardless of where we are, what we are doing, and how "well" we think we may or may not being doing it. We always do exactly what we are there to do, share the gift of ourselves, exactly how we are, in that exact moment!"

As we all begin, and continue, to consistently **know, own, live and share this truth; our own truth**, with the **peace** that it just is – (no matter who or what we think we are, need to be, what titles we have, what location we are in, who we are doing it with; that includes typical limitations we give ourselves like age, race, education, experience, and connections) - we will begin, and continue, to consistently live a life of peace, power and passion. We will live a life that is our own, guided by ourselves, and the source that lives within us, through the breath that moves through us. We will do so on our own terms, in our own divine 'time' and 'space'. We will begin to lose that time and space altogether. We will feel grounded in our flight, regardless of what lies beneath our feet.

That's what the Kaleidoscope is here to share with us, a reflection of the beauty within our souls, our unique puzzle piece. Its vision is here to share the truth of our individual souls, still intimately connected to the source with which they are.

Truth will reveal it's self to us all; over, and over again. It will reveal that which we do not see through the eyes looking back at us in the mirror. It will do so through the eyes of the relationships we find ourselves in; whether they are long lasting or the ones that peer across the counter at us for just a moment. And the truth of its reflection, the purpose in the process, will remain the same eyes opened or closed. It's our choice how we see and experience the Truth. That's the magic wand we all have in the palm of our hands, allowing us to craft the life we choose, how we choose.

In the end, the power of Truth is the power we all have, the power of ourselves, the power of the source rising within us, allowing us to create the life we choose on our terms. **All we have to do is unlearn everything we learned, in order to remember everything we already know!**

Again, the truth of you remains the same, eyes opened or closed; in all situations, in all relationships, at all 'times', in all 'spaces'. To know, own, live and share that Truth, your Truth, consciously allows you to create the live you choose, on your terms. It's freeing and powerful in a sense of which you cannot understand in those terms until you live them. And as of now, you can no longer go forward without seeing them, the eyes of truth, looking back at you each step of the way.

Your Center, Your Power, is revealed in the Kaleidoscope of your life allowing you to create the life you choose peacefully, passionately and powerfully! Welcome to its center!

The Campaign 4 Truth

The Campaign for Truth

The Campaign for Truth is a vision of perpetuating the truth, revealed here in 'Kaleidoscope', throughout our world. It's a zeal for peace, power and passion being spread from cell to cell, from individual to individual, until it's an infectious virus of epidemic proportions.

Might You Join Us?

Might you join us until the power of you and the power of me is realized in every soul on our planet. Until the Truth that:

**You already are all you need to be,
right where you are!**

Is the only truth we know!!

Where judgment sheds, and the love and acceptance we've always been is revealed!!

This is the campaign for truth.

**You already are all you need to be,
right where you are!**

We ask for your support. We ask for your action; the simple action of knowing, owning, living and then sharing the truth of YOU.

There are so many creative ways to do so. There are so many **simple acts that have grand impacts**.

Through our philosophy of "What You Think You Create!" you can, by simply doing four simple steps within in you and you alone, spread the truth of power throughout our planet. This one simple act can have a very grand impact on the peace, power and passion of an entire planet. . .

In your "little" moments simply

Know You
Own You
Live You
Share You

In that process, lived simply within you, *the Campaign for Truth* will become an infectious virus of epidemic proportions across our entire planet!

May we all live the truth, through our own expression of that truth:

"We already are all we need to be, right where we are."

Perpetuation Inspiration

There is no power like that of the deed it's self. The word simply inspires the deed within us to be lived around us.

The experience you have of the life you live will perpetuate the gift of peace, power and passion within you. Sharing the gift of you will extend that peace, power and passion to others.

Here are some simple ways you can join *the Campaign for Truth*. These are simple and intimate ways you can both share your truth, and perpetuate the gift of another finding their truth.

Share You
The simple and most basic way to share the truth is to share your own. Be the truth in all that you do. Remember that our little acts have grand impacts. Impacts we may not often see the other edge of.

So smile at the woman pouring your coffee. Extend a hand to someone who fell in front of you. Hold the door for the man behind you. Ask someone at the counter how their day is, look them in the eyes when you ask and listen with full presence no matter how long it takes. Let the driver move over in front of you. Pay the toll for the car behind you. Most importantly live this way daily.

Be present.
Stay connected.
Release judgment.
Find compassion.

Accept and Love.

Standing in your own strength allows others the space to stand in their own.

Stand Strong
Stand strong in your truth. Where ever you are not living your truth, in your life, begin transitioning into the light of truth. Take one step at a time. Just say yes. It's all that's required. The rest will take care of it's self.

You are responsible for ensuring you are in alignment with your truth, moment to moment. Life will carry its responsibility of communicating to you whenever you are out of alignment. Simply say yes in response to its opening. They are called indicators. They are openings. Some of these indicators will often feel like pain, sadness, fatigue, and many more like this. It may look like disease, rage, anger and violence. It can also look like apathy, or feel like loneliness. Life communicates in many fashions, just listen. You will know what is being said.

Stand Strong in the face of whatever appears in front of you. Stare directly into the eyes that are in front of you. See them. Accept them. And always be all of you looking back at them. Stand strong in your truth. Life supports you always.

Take Responsibility for You
Take responsibility for yourself. Let others take responsibility for them selves. *This is one of the greatest space creators I am currently aware of.*

Be keenly aware of when you are and are not taking responsibility for yourself; your perspectives, beliefs, choices, actions and results. Be keenly aware of when you are claiming responsibility that is not yours. Anytime this occurs, the space of another, and your self, is suffocating. Simply let go of the hold and trust in the one who is responsible. Remember they, too, are all they need to be, right where they are. Moreover, trust yourself. Simply share you, and receive the sharing of them, in a clear and open space.

Know, Own and Live You
Pick up our workbook, *Your Center, Your Power*. Define your essence. Shed all that covers you revealing the truth of you. The You that is as unique as a snowflake. The You that has always been there. The You that you already are in every moment of your life. Reveal your "Brand Statement", the one tag line that communicates You. Then be conscious of the process of owning and living it.

Most importantly use this process daily until it becomes you.

Replicate, then Perpetuate:
Purchase *Kaleidoscope* online at www.lulu.com. Then share it with at least one person. Inside the book sign your name. Write your story, your truth, maybe the inspired wisdom you have to share in a comment or two. Perpetuate it by sharing it with one person. Ask that person to replicate the signature, and their truth, story or wisdom. Ask them to perpetuate it, paying it and the process forward to another person as well.

Chain Replication:
A variation is to also ask the individual you share this book with to purchase a book themselves and begin one more strain of replication perpetuation. Then sit back and imagine the strands of replication. Imagine the ripples of truth and power you are sending into the world. Paying forward, might you imagine. . . the power found in the truth of ourselves gifted to others.

Simply Give
Simply purchase and give the book, share the experience with one other person. Remember simple acts have grand impacts.

Have Fun with Giving
Give the book, *Kaleidoscope* to someone you do not know.

The man sitting next to you on the plane. The young adult pouring your coffee at Starbucks. The pregnant woman you just walked by. The teacher of your children. The nanny who tends to your little people. The one who funds your pay check. The driver of the bus you commute on.

Moreover, have fun wondering and ultimately knowing the joy they might get. Be mystified by the impact your small act might have upon the grandness of who they already are.

Get Creative
We are creative souls, an extension of the energy of creation it's self. Just do whatever comes to you. Get creative. Do whatever action is inspired within to spread and share the truth with others. The synergy

of our combined action, linked in our common intention will create an infectious virus of epidemic proportions. . .

So listen, trust your self, and take action grounded in sharing and the rest will follow naturally.

Perpetuate Your Campaign
Inspire action in others! Get online at www.Campaign4Truth.com and share your creative campaign for spreading the truth! Tell us what you are doing to help us create an infectious virus of epidemic proportions, one that infects others with peace, power and passion, one that spreads the truth that, *You already are all you need to be, right where you are!*

Bibliography

Bouble, Michael *Home.* Album: It's Time, Reprise, 2005.

Gafni, Marc *Soul Prints.* New York: Fireside, Simon and Schuster, 2001.

Nelson, Willie *On The Road Again.* Album: On The Road Again, Columbia River Entertainment, 2001.

Zukav, Gary *The Seat of the Soul.* New York: Fireside, Simon and Shuster, 1989.

Images

The Kaleidoscopes seen in this book are offered and produced by Echo Earth Galleries; a gallery of peace, love and light. More can been seen of this marvelous work at www.echoearth.com. They are works of Fred Casselman. We honor he, and his wonderous work. We thank him for sharing his vision, his love and his images.

About the Author

ShannonRae

Writer, poet, speaker, ordained minister, business owner, consultant, social activist, mother, friend, sister, daughter, passionate woman. . .

This powerful, poetic woman is captivating! Her words are precise, her presence electrifying and her wisdom inspiring. Her range is vast; translating the same wisdom to Fortune 500 companies and small groups, men and women, adults and children.

No matter how you connect with this woman, transmutation will occur, creating exponential results in your life and business!

The Power Integration Center has enabled her to integrate three major themes in her life; business success, spirit and people. Her undergraduate degree in Human Development, graduate degree in Organizational Effectiveness and most importantly, intuition about people, enable her to support individuals and organizations in achieving their greatest potential, rooted in their core essence. She combines this with 10+ years of successful business experience and a connection to Spirit, creating unprecedented productivity improvements for her clients and/or their companies.

Shannon has published the book *Your Center, Your Power* along with several products for business and personal growth. She has founded and directs the Power Integration Center, a community where people connect to peace, power and passion. Its mission is to create planetary peace by raising people's individual personal power and then connecting them together through grass roots communities!

Speaking on business, empowerment and spiritual issues, Shannon will inspire you to create consistent, conscious results grounded in your core essence. She has created results from clarity of purpose, passionate meaning and fulfillment for small independent business owners, to 800% revenue growth in six months for multi-million dollar businesses. She speaks with, as well as works with businesses, individuals and large groups of people who are RAW: Ready, Accepting, and Willing to live who they already are!

People walk away wondering how a woman at such an age and size can inspire so much power, creating such grand results in others, organizations and herself. Shannon means small and wise. She is wise enough to know size, time and space are only limitations if we choose them to be.

www.ingramcontent.com/pod-product-compliance
Lightning Source LLC
Chambersburg PA
CBHW021224090426
42740CB00006B/377